## Introduction & Symbols

Let me introduce us. I'm Christine Schwenck Cardaci and my husband is Thomas Cardaci. We met while both working at the West Long Branch Post Office in New Jersey as Letter Carriers in early 1988. We got married in 1991 and had our wedding photos taken at the Twin Lights of Navesink in Highlands, New Jersey. Who would have ever guessed that years later that would become so ironic? We both love to travel to different states and provinces. We fell in love with lighthouses in September 1996 while vacationing in Nova Scotia, Canada. We became hooked and it began our quest to see as many as we could. We enjoy the adventure and the challenge that each vacation day brings. We still have many more to see. This is a great way to see parts of our beautiful world.

When we first started lighthouse hunting, we never thought that it would consume us as much as it did. We worked together at the Post Office for 18 ½ years before I left. Hopefully Tommy will be able to retire soon. This way we can devote all of our time to the series of photographic books we plan to write. It is exciting to find something that makes us and others happy. Sharing our knowledge and experiences of the lighthouses is very fulfilling. We hope you find this list helpful on your lighthouse quest. The photos in this book have been taken by Christine & Tommy Cardaci and all are copy written. Most of the lighthouses listed in our book are available as color prints. www.TheLighthouseHunters.com

When we were on our many vacations to the different provinces and states, we would have loved to have a list like this one. We spent too many hours to count flipping through many different books and maps just to find or not find a lighthouse. We hope this helps all of the other fellow lighthouse enthusiasts. We hope to see you out there!

We've come up with an easy system for everyone to follow. We've broken down each lighthouse into 5 categories. We also broke down the hikes into e-easy, m-medium, h-hard, and x-extreme. This easy key will help you to identify the categories of each of the lighthouses.

|  | |
|---|---|
| Car | 🚗 |
| Hike | 🚶 |
| Boat | ⛵ |
| Ferry | 🚢 |
| Air | ✈ |

Going to many of the lighthouses are as easy as driving right up to them. Some you have to make a little more effort, but it's worth it. Some hikes are much more time-consuming. Others require a quick passenger or car ferry ride to an island. The boat trips are a little more complicated sometimes because of everyone's schedules and of course the weather. Then there's the helicopter or private plane which can be expensive and for some people like me, scary. Everything all depends on the individual person. So grab a friend and go!

# Maine

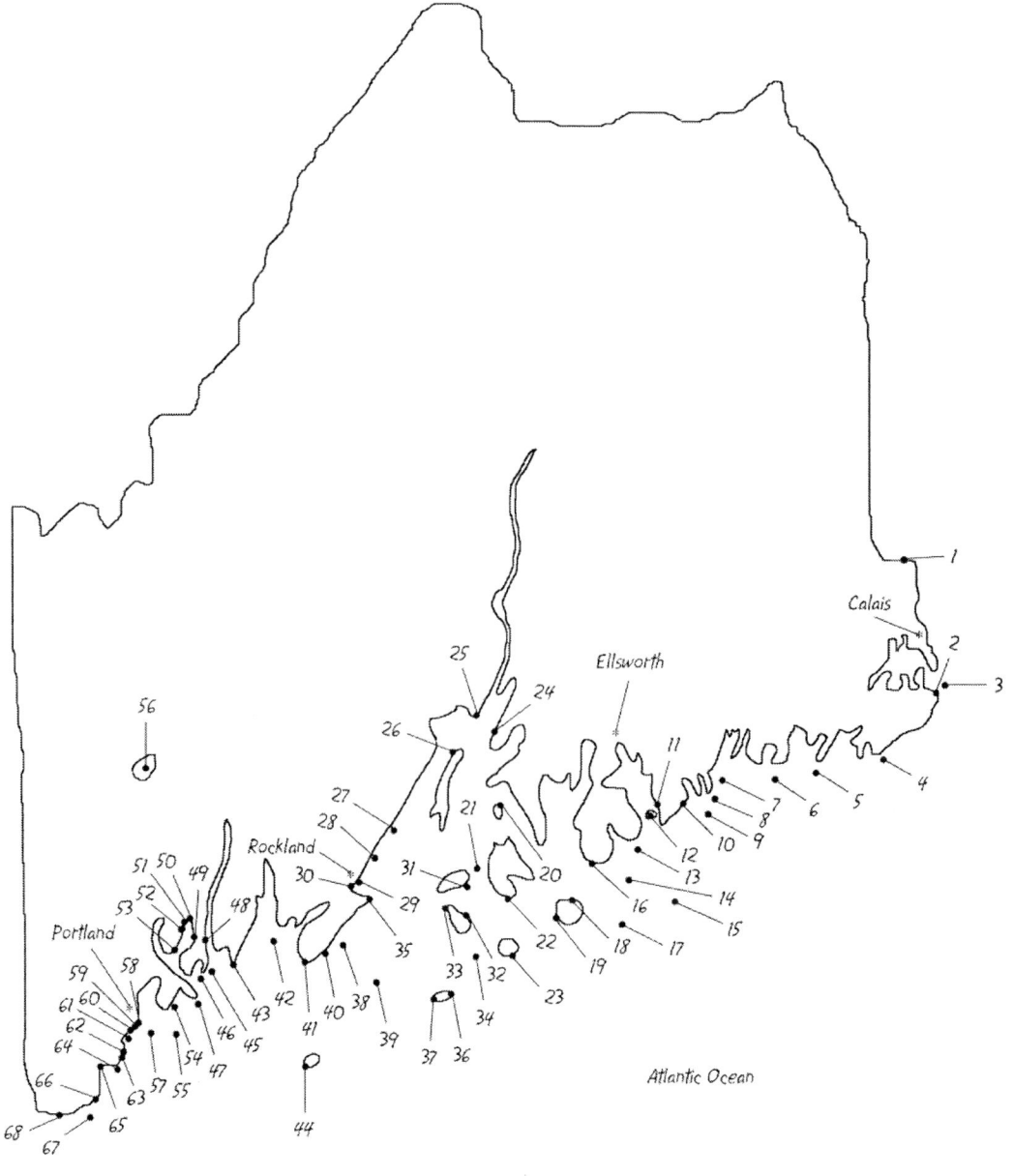

Calais
Ellsworth
Rockland
Portland
Atlantic Ocean

59.   Taken on 9-28-00

60.   Taken on 9-28-00

2.   Taken on 9-22-98

# Maine

1. 🚗 Whitlock's Mill
2. 🚗 West Quoddy Head
3. 🚗 Lubec Channel
4. ⛵ Little River
5. ⛵ Libby Island
6. ⛵ Moose Peak
7. ⛵ Nash Island
8. ⛵ Narraguagus/Pond Island
9. ⛵ Petit Manan
10. 🚗 Prospect Harbor Point
11. 🚗 Winter Harbor
12. ⛵ Egg Rock
13. 🚢 Bear Island
14. 🚢 Baker Island
15. ⛵ Mount Desert Rock
16. 🚗 Bass Harbor Head
17. ⛵ Great Duck Island
18. 🚢 Burnt Coat Harbor/Hockamock Head
19. ✈ Blue Hill Bay/Eggemoggin
20. 🚗 Pumpkin Island
21. ⛵ Eagle Island
22. ⛵ Deer Island Thorofare/Mark Island
23. ⛵ Isle Au Haut
24. 🚗 Dice Head/Dyce Head
25. 🚗 Fort Point
26. 🚢 Grindle Point
27. 🚗 Curtis Island
28. ⛵ Indian Island
29. 🚶 m Rockland Breakwater
30. 🚗 Rockland Harbor Southwest
31. ⛵ Goose Rock
32. ⛵ Brown's Head
33. ⛵ Heron Neck
34. ⛵ Saddleback Ledge
35. 🚗 Owl's Head
36. ⛵ Matinicus Rock North
37. ⛵ Matinicus Rock South
38. ⛵ Whitehead Island
39. ⛵ Two Bush Island

9. Taken on 9-30-04

16. Taken on 9-30-04

26. Taken on 9-24-98

## Maine continued

| | | |
|---|---|---|
| 40. | ⛵ | Tenants Harbor |
| 41. | 🚗 | Marshall Point |
| 42. | ⛵ | Franklin Island |
| 43. | 🚗 | Pemaquid Point |
| 44. | ⛵ | Monhegan Island |
| 45. | 🚗 | Ram Island |
| 46. | ⛵ | Burnt Island |
| 47. | 🚗 | The Cuckolds |
| 48. | 🚗 | Hendricks Head |
| 49. | 🚗 | Perkins Island |
| 50. | 🚗 | Doubling Point/Kennebec River |
| 51. | 🚗 | Doubling Point Front Range |
| 52. | 🚗 | Doubling Point Rear Range |
| 53. | 🚗 | Squirrel Point |
| 54. | ⛵ | Pond Island |
| 55. | ⛵ | Sequin Island |
| 56. | ⛵ | Ladies Delight |
| 57. | ⛵ | Halfway Rock |
| 58. | 🚗 | Portland Breakwater/Petroleum Docks |
| 59. | 🚗 | Spring Point Ledge |
| 60. | 🚗 | Portland Head |
| 61. | 🚗 | Ram Island Ledge |
| 62. | 🚗 | Cape Elizabeth East/Two Lights |
| 63. | 🚗 | Cape Elizabeth West/Two Lights |
| 64. | 🚶 e | Wood Island |
| 65. | ⛵ | Goat Island |
| 66. | 🚗 | Cape Neddick/The Nubble |
| 67. | ⛵ | Boon Island |
| 68. | 🚗 | Whaleback Ledge |

44. Taken on 9-27-99

50. Taken on 6-21-99

68. Taken on 9-21-03

# New Hampshire

1. 🚗 Portsmouth Harbor/New Castle
2. ⛵ Isle of Shoals/White Island
3. ⛵ Herrick Cove
4. ⛵ Loon Island
5. ⛵ Burkhaven

* — Grantham

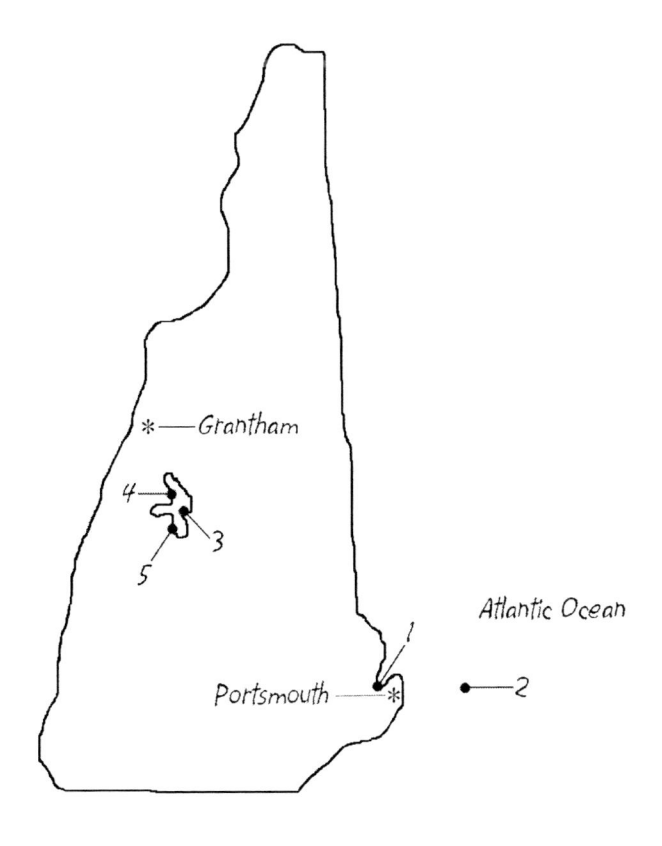

Atlantic Ocean

Portsmouth

2. Taken on 10-2-04

1. Taken on 9-21-03

# Massachusetts

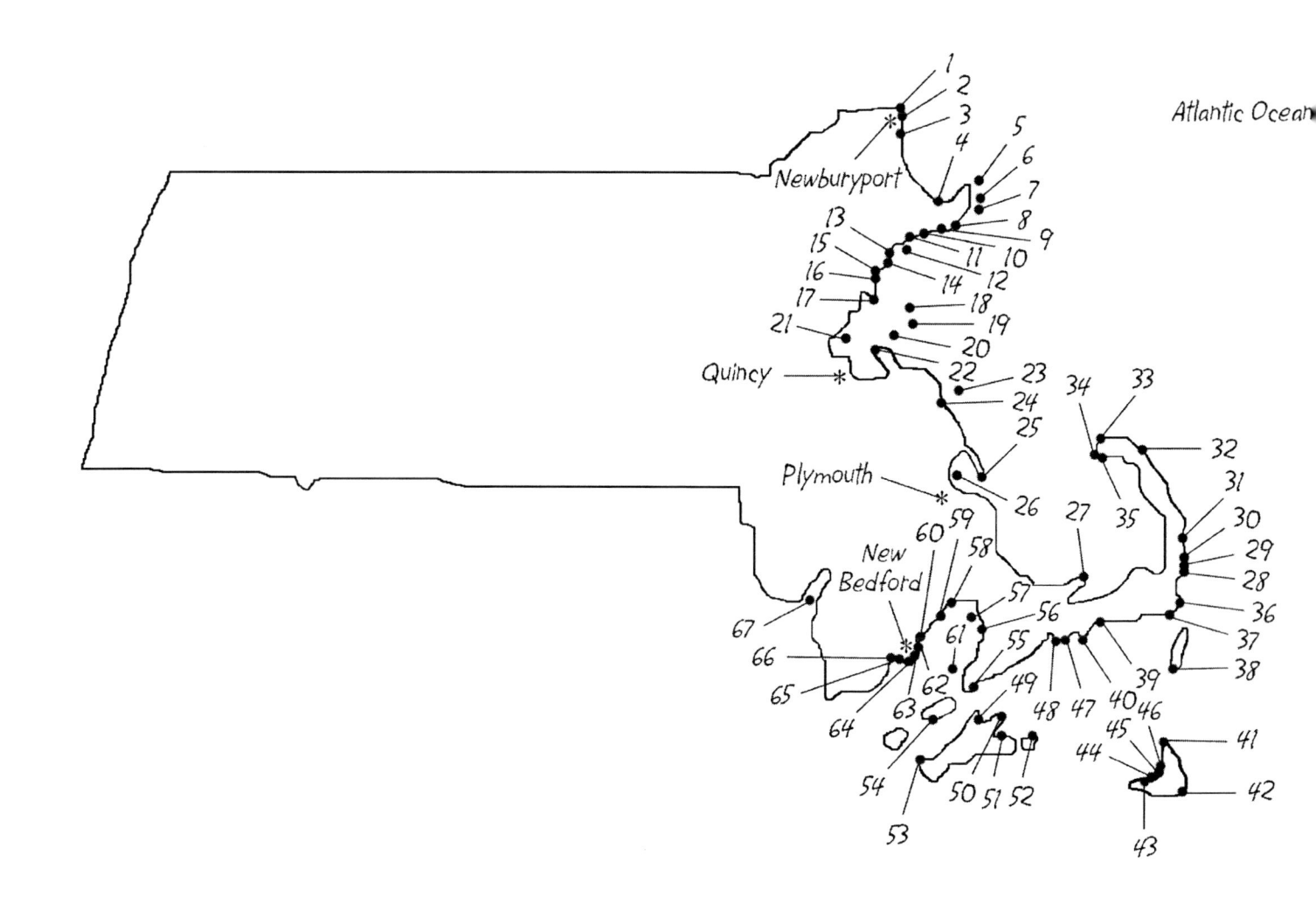

Atlantic Ocean

Newburyport

Quincy

Plymouth

New Bedford

18.  Taken on 5-17-03

32.  Taken on 6-10-98

52.  Taken on 10-6-04

# Massachusetts

1. 🚗 Newburyport Front Range
2. 🚗 Newburyport Rear Range
3. 🚗 Newburyport Harbor/Plum Island
4. 🚗 Annisquam/Wigwam Point
5. ⛵ Straitsmouth Island/Straitsmouth Harbor
6. ⛵ Cape Ann
7. ⛵ Thacher's Island North
8. 🚗 Eastern Point
9. 🚗 Gloucester Breakwater
10. ⛵ Ten Pound Island
11. 🚗 Coastal Observation Tower
12. ⛵ Baker's Island
13. 🚗 Hospital Point Front Range
14. 🚗 Hospital Point Rear Range
15. 🚗 Fort Pickering/Winter Island
16. 🚗 Derby Wharf
17. 🚗 Marblehead
18. ⛵ Graves Ledge
19. ⛵ Boston Harbor
20. ⛵ Nix's Mate
21. ⛵ Deer Island
22. ⛵ Long Island Head
23. ⛵ Minot's Ledge
24. 🚗 Scituate
25. ⛵ Plymouth/Gurnet Point
26. ⛵ Duxbury Pier
27. 🚗 Sandy Neck
28. 🚗 Three Sisters-1
29. 🚗 Three Sisters-2
30. 🚗 Three Sisters-3
31. 🚗 Nauset Beach
32. 🚗 Highland/Cape Cod
33. 🚶 m Race Point
34. 🚶 m Wood End
35. 🚶 m Long Point
36. 🚗 Chatham
37. 🚶 m Stage Harbor
38. ⛵ Monomoy Point
39. 🚗 Bass River/West Dennis

4. Taken on 6-12-98

19. Taken on 5-17-03

24. Taken on 9-29-00

## Massachusetts continued

40. Point Gammon
41. Great Point/Nantucket
42. Sankaty Head
43. Cliff Front Range
44. Cliff Rear Range
45. Old Brant Point
46. Brant Point
47. Hyannis Port
48. Hyannis Harbor
49. West Chop
50. East Chop/Telegraph Hill
51. Edgartown Harbor
52. Cape Poge/Cape Pogue
53. Gay Head
54. Tarpaulin Cove
55. Nobska Point
56. Wing's Neck
57. Cleveland East Ledge
58. Lightship Nantucket II/WLV-613
59. Bird Island
60. Ned's Point
61. Buzzard's Bay Entrance
62. Palmer Island
63. Clark's Point
64. Butler's Flats
65. Lightship New Bedford/LV-114/WAL-116
66. Lightship Nantucket I/WLV-612
67. Borden Flats

36. Taken on 10-7-04

42. Taken on 9-23-99

60. Taken on 6-9-98

# Our Northeast Hunts

We've been to Maine, New Hampshire and Massachusetts numerous times over the years. We've researched many charters or private excursions and we've been able to get on a few. We were on the Duck Harbor Cruise ferry and we were able to photograph the lighthouses from the boat. On the Swans Island Ferry we saw two lighthouses with our car. In July 2004 we took the long holiday weekend and drove 6 ½ hours to Camden, Maine. The cruise the following morning lasted 6 ½ hours. We were able to get much closer to the lights; what a difference! While in Wells, Maine visit The Lighthouse Depot, the only place I like to shop. In Millbridge, Maine we set up a 37 mile three-hour boat trip with Jamie of Robertson Sea Tours to see Petit Manan, Narraguagus-Pond Island and Nash Island. We had a great voyage. Eventually, we will be seeing some Maine lights by air.

There's a fantastic five-hour lighthouse cruise that travels around Boston Harbor. We traveled 60 nautical miles to see the dozen lighthouses right after a Nor'easter had hit. We had choppy seas and strong winds but later the thick clouds gave way to beautiful sunshine. From this cruise, we were able to get closer to the lights. We had a good day except for getting sea sick. I even took the seasick pills but the huge six to eight foot swells got to me. I wanted to jump overboard! So for the first half of the trip, I struggled to take my photos. It took all of my energy to pick up my head from the table. I'm sure there are many people out there who can relate to this story. Later, I was able to enjoy the trip as the seas calmed down.

Our first time in Martha's Vineyard and Nantucket was in September 1999. In Nantucket, we rented a taxi to take us to the lighthouses because we forgot our driver's licenses and we couldn't rent a car. We had only 3 hours on the island and our driver was inexperienced. We didn't have any directions to aid the driver so we ended up missing one. The next day in Martha's Vineyard we rented a maroon 4-wheel drive Jeep for four-hours. At this time we were told that we couldn't drive on the long beach to get to the one lighthouse. We got to our first light and Tommy realized he had only one out of three lenses. We were shocked and decided to ask another lighthouse buff to borrow his lenses. Later I asked to drive the Jeep, and when I got in, all the instrument lights went on and the truck wouldn't work. Tommy got back in and everything was fine, of course. On the way back to the ferry, I spotted the distant Cape Poge light on the long beach. When I went to get out of the truck, I took a fall into the gutter. I was really scraped up and the camcorder went into the sand. We never had this many mishaps in our lives and all these were in a few days. Pretty weird. Luckily, years later our trip went much more smoothly. On Wednesday, October 6, 2004, my 39th birthday, we took the early Steamship Authority ferry to Martha's Vineyard. We went on a tour with the Trustees of Reservations to see the Cape Poge light and got to climb up inside. The next day we got on the Steamship Authority-Flying Cloud fast ferry to Nantucket. We also went on a tour with the Trustees of Reservations to see the Great Point light. We had great weather for these two days.

In Provincetown we did the 4-mile round trip walk to see both lights on the tip of Cape Cod. In June 1998 we walked there and it was hot. We were much more comfortable in the fall of 2004 because it was windy and cool. Our next stop was to see Race Point lighthouse. We got our permit so we could take our 4x4 on the beach. Every car must have a shovel, plywood, tow strap, jack, spare tire, and tire gauge to travel on the soft sand.

# Rhode Island

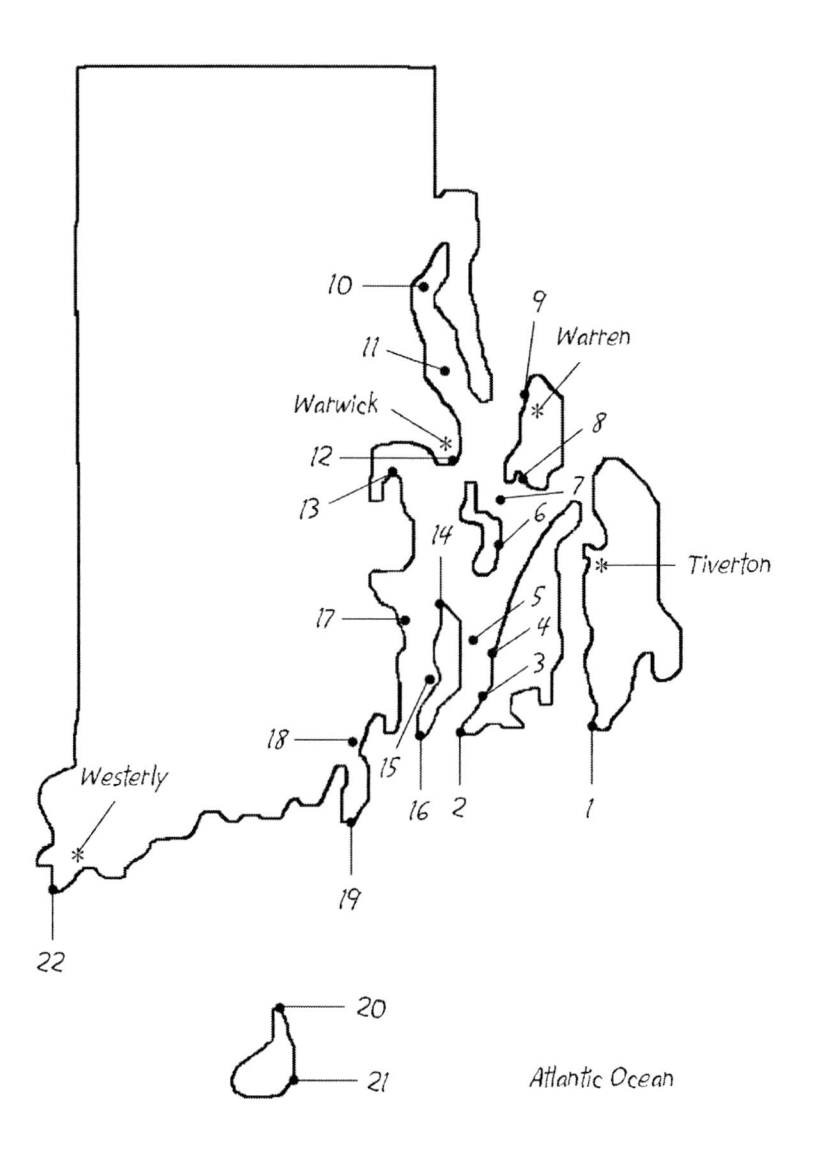

2.  Taken on 6-9-98

20. Taken on 9-21-99

17. Taken on 10-3-04

# Rhode Island

1. ⛵ Sakonnet Shoal
2. 🚗 Castle Hill
3. 🚗 Ida Lewis Rock/Lime Rock
4. 🚗 Newport Harbor/Goat Island
5. 🚗 Rose Island
6. ⛵ Prudence Island/Sandy Point
7. ⛵ Hog Island Shoal
8. 🚗 Bristol Ferry
9. 🚗 Nayatt Point
10. 🚶 e Pomham Rocks
11. 🚢 Conimicut Shoal
12. 🚗 Warwick
13. 🚗 Poplar Point
14. ⛵ Conanicut Island/North Light
15. 🚗 Dutch Island
16. 🚗 Beavertail
17. 🚗 Plum Beach
18. 🚗 Gooseberry Island
19. 🚗 Point Judith
20. 🚢 🚶 m Block Island North
21. 🚢 🚗 Block Island Southeast
22. 🚗 Watch Hill

6. Taken on 10-12-02

16. Taken on 10-3-04

12

# Connecticut

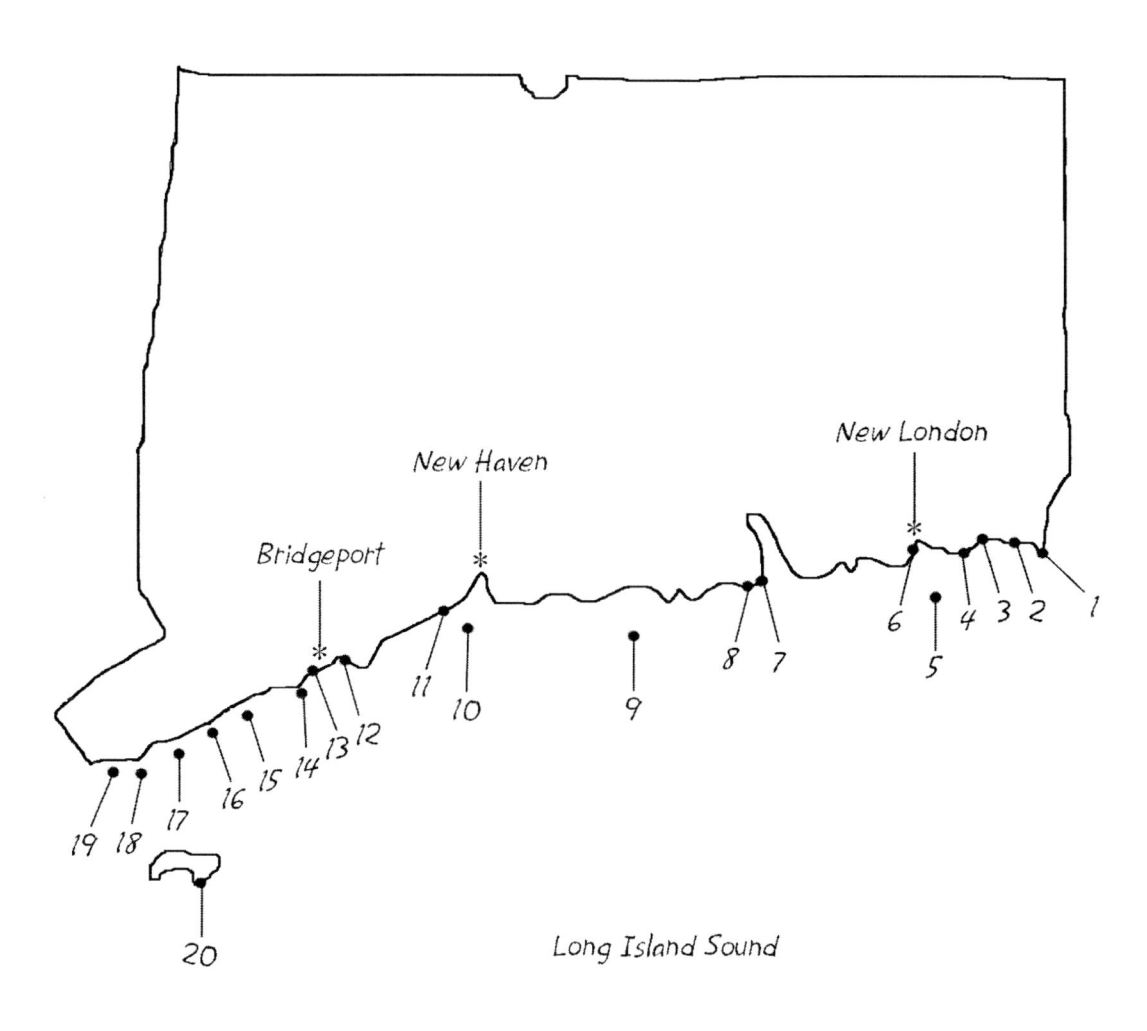

New London
New Haven
Bridgeport

Long Island Sound

5.   Taken on 9-20-99         17.   Taken on 6-15-04         1.   Taken on 10-9-04

# Connecticut

1. 🚗 Stonington Harbor/Stonington Old Museum
2. 🚗 Mystic Seaport
3. 🚗 Morgan Point
4. 🚗 Avery Point
5. 🚢 New London Ledge
6. 🚗 New London Harbor
7. 🚶 m Saybrook Breakwater/Old Saybrook
8. 🚗 Lynde Point
9. ⛵ Faulkner Island
10. 🚶 m Southwest Ledge/New Haven Breakwater
11. 🚗 New Haven Harbor/Five Mile Point
12. 🚗 Stratford Point
13. 🚗 Tongue Point/Bridgeport Breakwater
14. 🚶 e Fayerweather Island/Black Rock Harbor
15. ⛵ Penfield Reef
16. ⛵ Peck's Ledge
17. ⛵ Sheffield Island/Norwalk
18. ⛵ Green's Ledge
19. ⛵ Stamford Harbor/Chatham Rock
20. ⛵ Great Captain Island

11. Taken on 9-26-04

16. Taken on 6-15-04

# Lower New York

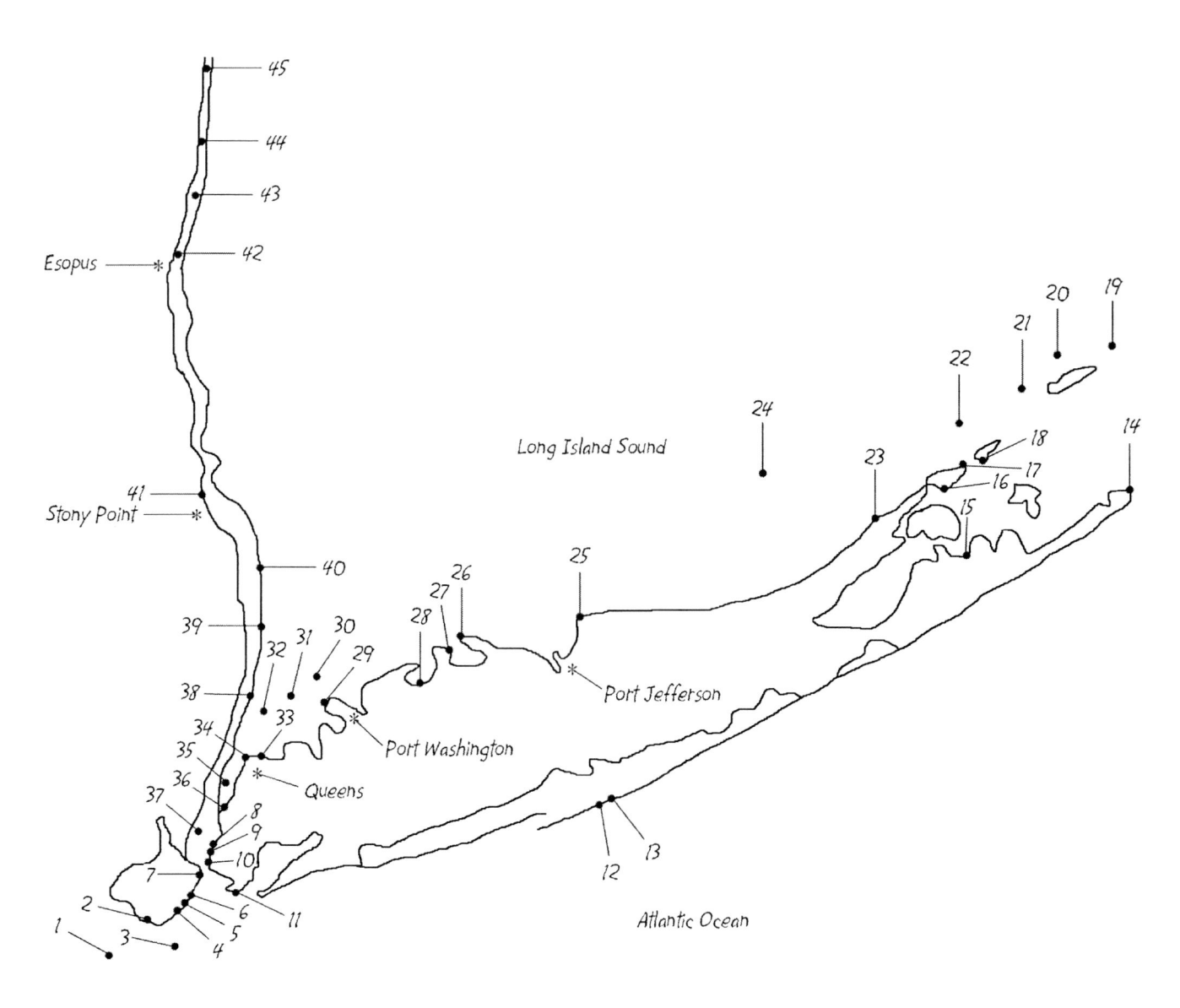

*Esopus*

*Stony Point*

Long Island Sound

*Port Jefferson*

*Port Washington*

*Queens*

Atlantic Ocean

13.   Taken on 3-11-06

43.   Taken on 6-9-01

14.   Taken on 3-11-06

## Lower New York

1. ⚐ Old Orchard Shoal
2. 🚗 Princess Bay/Prince's Bay
3. ⚐ West Bank Front Range
4. 🚗 Staten Island Rear Range
5. 🚗 New Dorp/Swash Channel Rear Range
6. 🚗 Elm Tree Front Range/Swash Channel Front Range
7. 🚗 Fort Wadsworth
8. 🚗 Lightship Ambrose/LV-87/WAL-512
9. 🚗 Lightship Nantucket/LV-112/WAL-534
10. 🚗 Titanic Memorial
11. 🚗 Coney Island/Norton Point
12. 🚗 Fire Island Monument
13. 🚶 e Fire Island/Winking Woman
14. 🚗 Montauk Point
15. 🚶 m Cedar Island/Cedar Point
16. ⚐ Long Beach Bar
17. 🚗 Orient Point/Old Coffee Pot
18. ⚐ Plum Island/Plum Gut
19. ⚐ Latimer Reef
20. ⚐ North Dumpling
21. ⚐ Race Rock/Long Island Reef
22. ⚐ Little Gull
23. 🚗 Horton Point
24. ⚐ Stratford Shoal
25. 🚗 Old Field Point
26. 🚗 Eaton's Neck
27. 🚗 Lloyd Harbor/Huntington Harbor
28. ⚐ Cold Springs Harbor
29. ⚐ Sand's Point
30. ⚐ Execution Rocks
31. ⚐ Stepping Stones
32. ⚐ Throg's Neck
33. 🚗 Whitestone Point
34. ⚐ North Brother Island
35. 🚗 Blackwell Island/Welfare Island
36. 🚗 H. W. Wilson
37. 🚗 Statue of Liberty
38. 🚗 Lightship Fryingpan Shoal/LV-115/WAL-537
39. 🚶 m Jeffrey's Hook/George Washington Bridge light

4. Taken on 6-4-00

17. Taken on 8-10-05

39. Taken on 5-17-03

## Lower New York continued

40. 🚕 Tarrytown/Kingsland Point
41. 🚶 e Stony Point
42. 🚕 Esopus Meadows/Maid of the Meadow
43. 🚶 e Rondout Two/Kingston/ Rondout Creek
44. 🚶 e Saugerties
45. 🚕 Hudson City/Hudson-Athens

41. Taken on 6-7-00

# Our Mid-Atlantic Hunts

We've been to Rhode Island, Connecticut, Lower New York, New Jersey (our home state), and Delaware many times. We took a lighthouse cruise out of Rhode Island a few years ago. The boat had prop trouble and the weather was horrible. The cruise should have been canceled because it was difficult to take shots. Not our best time. The best lighthouse cruise was out of southern New Jersey aboard the Cape May Whale Watcher. We saw seven off-shore lighthouses up close on this perfect day in August 2001. We were even given a great buffet that included shrimp cocktail. This was well worth the trip.

We've visited the Hudson River lights in the heat of the summer and in the snowy winter. One day we would like to get closer to them by boat. We've driven all over the coast of Long Island to photograph the lighthouses. We plan to revisit soon to improve our shots.

We took four days in June 2004 on our 30' Hunter sailboat up to Connecticut and Long Island, NY. We moored in Manhasset Bay in Port Washington, NY for the night. Near Stamford Harbor, CT our water pump belt broke on the boat. This delay affected how far we could go in Connecticut. We were able to see only a few lighthouses off-shore and it was time to turn around and head home. We took many shots of the off-shore lights in the East River of New York and went under the nine bridges. We were able to get fairly close to the Statue of Liberty. We got all the way home safely but not without a few stories. We improved our shots tremendously.

Generally we don't plan vacations for the middle of the summer for a few reasons. An opportunity arose and we decided to take a few days in August 2005. On Wednesday, we got up early so we could drive the three hours to Connecticut. The cruise to the Connecticut and New York off-shore lights was with Captain John's Sport Fishing Center. It was a five-hour trip through Long Island Sound. We had a nice blue sky and we felt the heat and humidity only when we stopped to take our shots. We were very happy because we had a wonderful trip! We even met a fellow Letter Carrier from Pennsylvania who also loves lighthouses. Thursday, we left from home early again and drove the 2 ¼ hours down to Cape May, New Jersey. The lighthouse would have been nicer if the haze wasn't around. I took some beautiful shots from the beach with the dune grass. After a few more lighthouses we drove back home. Friday, began the same as Thursday, but this time we took the Cape May-Lewes car ferry and we barely felt the heat index of 105°. We were told that the southbound ferry was going to go right past the two off-shore breakwater lights in Delaware. The southbound trip was 1 ¼ hours and the last fifteen minutes was when the lights were at their closest. Too bad they were still one mile away. We later found out that the northbound ferry is the one that goes right in-between the two lights. Obviously, that ferry would have been the one to take. There's always next year. We had haze problems, too, and if we were told about the other boat getting closer, the haze wouldn't have been as much of a factor. We saw a few more repeat lights in Delaware before heading home the next day.

Be sure and visit our website for purchasing color photographs of the United States lighthouses and for more copies of our American travel book. www.TheLighthouseHunters.com

# New Jersey

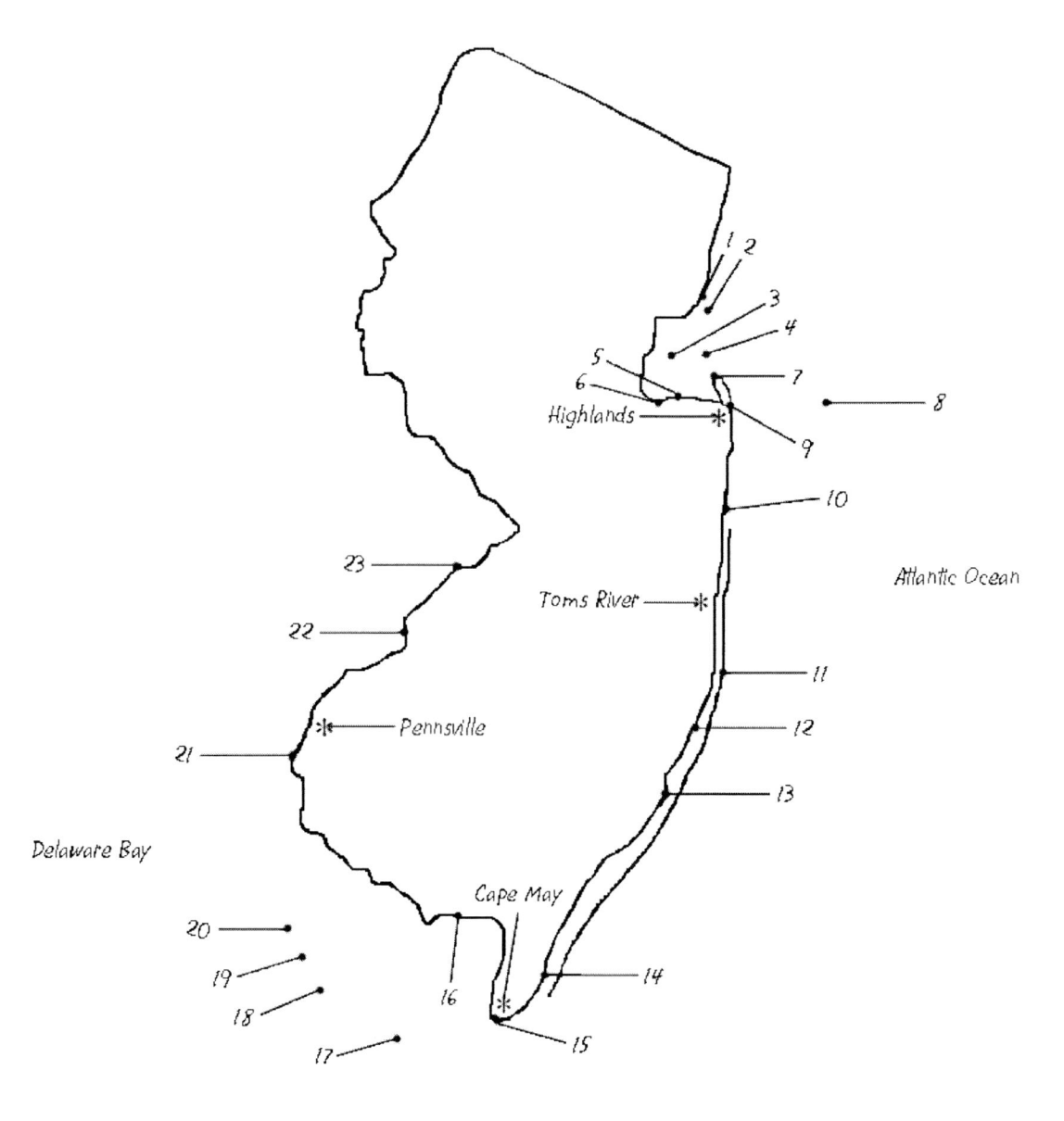

Highlands
Toms River
Atlantic Ocean
Pennsville
Delaware Bay
Cape May

11.  Taken on 2-15-04
17.  Taken on 8-3-01 
7.  Taken on 4-9-05

## New Jersey

1. 🚗 Lightship Winter Quarter/LV-107/WAL-529
2. ⛴ Robbin's Reef/Katie's Light
3. ⛴ Great Beds/Great Kills
4. ⛴ Romer Shoal
5. 🚗 Conover Beacon/Conover Front Range
6. 🚗 Chapel Hill Rear Range
7. 🚗 Sandy Hook
8. ⛴ Ambrose Channel
9. 🚗 Twin Lights of Navesink
10. 🚗 Sea Girt
11. 🚗 Barnegat
12. 🚗 Tuckerton Replica
13. 🚗 Absecon
14. 🚗 Hereford Inlet
15. 🚗 Cape May
16. 🚗 East Point/Maurice River
17. ⛴ Brandywine Shoal
18. ⛴ Miah Maull Shoal
19. ⛴ Elbow of Cross Ledge
20. ⛴ Ship John Shoal
21. 🚗 Finn's Point Rear Range/Fort Mott
22. 🚗 Tinicum Rear Range
23. 🚗 Lightship Barnegat/LV-79/WAL-506

5. Taken on 2-25-04

22. Taken on 2-18-01

# Delaware

1. 🚗 Marcus Hook Front Range
2. 🚗 Marcus Hook Rear Range
3. 🚗 Bellevue Rear Range
4. 🚗 Liston Front Range
5. 🚗 Liston Rear Range
6. 🚗 Reedy Island Rear Range
7. 🚗 Cape Henlopen
8. ⛵ Fourteen Foot Bank
9. 🚗 Delaware Breakwater East/Delaware Inner Breakwater
10. 🚗 Harbor of Refuge/Harbor of Refuge South Breakwater
11. 🚗 Lightship Overfalls/LV-118/WAL-539
12. 🚗 Cape Henlopen Replica
13. 🚗 Fenwick Island

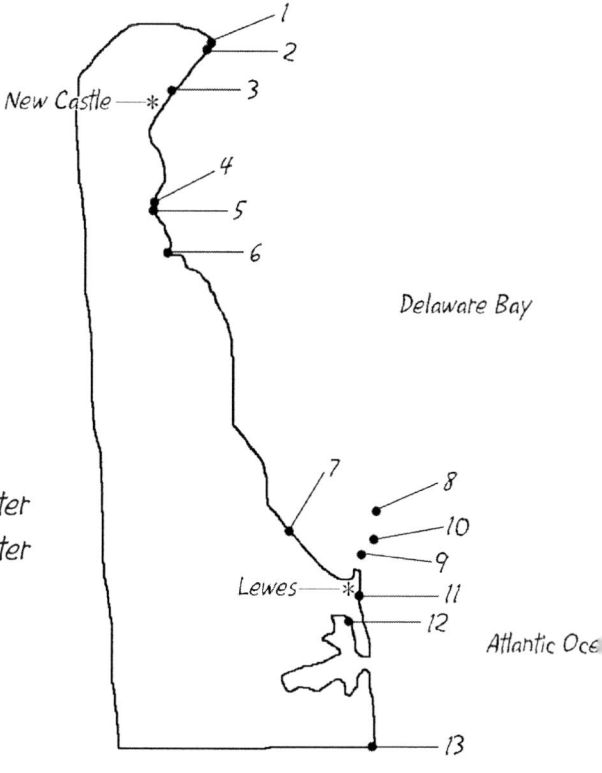

8. Taken on 8-3-01

13. Taken on 4-23-02

5. Taken 4-26-02

**Alliance for a Living Ocean**
528 Dock Street
Beach Haven, NJ 08008
Tel: (609) 492-0222

## Our 20th Anniversary
*"Continuing our years of environmental advocacy and education into the future"*

**To our Members and Supporters:**

2007 is ALO's 20th anniversary, and it is also a "watershed" year for our organization. It is a time to celebrate our past, and it is a time to renew and rebuild ALO for its future mission. The health of the world's environment is now center stage, and ALO will be there to do its part to protect our ocean environment.

The exciting news is that our new ALO office and gift shop will open the first week of July following the dedication of the State of New Jersey Maritime Museum. The museum is located at the end of Dock Street opposite the Boat House and the Ketch restaurants in Beach Haven. Our office is on the second floor and the gift shop is on the main floor. The museum building is wonderful, **please** come and visit us. All these changes did not come without some pain and suffering. As we all know, changing locations is not easy. Hundreds of hours of work were involved in moving computers, files, office and program supplies, and all the gift shop inventory. But taking care of ALO's material possessions was not the biggest concern. It was our people. ALO was, after all, an organization that ran on people power. It was with extremely sad hearts that ALO said goodbye to so many of our faithful staff and volunteers. They were friends as well as helpers. Our long time Director, Carol Elliott, moved with her family and now lives in Cape May. Our dedicated staff members moved on to full time employment or retirement. Just as crushing a blow is that we lost so many of our volunteers to relocation, illness and death. They all are sorely missed.

With that said, ALO is moving forward. Because of the uncertainty and delays, we could not get the office fully operational on time. As a result, ALO could only schedule a limited set of programs for the summer of 2007. Here are the programs that we are planning for this summer:

**Seining at the Bay,** Tuesdays, 10-11:15 am
July 17, 24, 31 and Aug 7
Ship Bottom Bay Beach (Beach Arlington)

**Inlet Lore.** Fridays, 10-11 am
July 13, 20, 27 and Aug 3
Barnegat Light State Park, 1st Pavilion

**Stories by the Sea,** Mondays, 10:30 am
July 16, 23, 30 and August 6
At ALO office, Maritime Museum, BH

**International Coastal Cleanup**
September 15th
Call ALO for more information

ALO was unable to update its website for the past 1/2 year, and we apologize for the inconvenience. You can now check the event schedule at "www.livingocean.org/events" for any last minute changes.

If ALO is to accomplish all that is planned, we need your help! We need people to work as volunteers in both the office and the shop, and we need your monetary support. Your donations will be used strictly for educational programs, newsletters, and staff support. With the generous help of the Maritime Museum, we are no longer burdened by rent and utility payments. The ALO Board is asking you to support our Renewal Fund for 2007. A new membership drive will be mounted at the beginning of the 2008 year. **ALO is looking forward! Please look forward with us. Thanks again for your past support.**

---

ALO's Renewal Campaign — Please return to ALO at 528 Dock Street, Beach Haven, NJ 08008.

NAME_____PHONE_____
STREET ADDRESS_____
CITY, STATE and ZIP_____
Donation Amount_____     I would like to Volunteer_____

# Our Southern Hunts

For two days in late September 2002, we went back down to Maryland for a lighthouse cruise. We saw ten off-shore lights up close traveling 110 nautical miles in 7 ½ hours. In April 2003, we took two weeks off from work. We had to modify our plans due to snow and now we had only a ten-day trip. We drove straight to Florida in the pouring rain and worked our way north. This was a good move because we had beautiful blue skies for the whole trip. Florida's East Coast is where we began, followed by Georgia. We saw half of the lighthouses in South Carolina. In North Carolina, we were able to get on every ferry and boat needed to see all lights on the mainland and the Outer Banks. The passenger ferry to Bald Head took only twenty-five minutes one way and there was a short walk to the light. After getting back to the mainland, a car ferry took us from Southport to Fort Fisher. As soon as the ferry pulled away, we were able to see another lighthouse. Next we had a great little trip to see Cape Lookout by taking a small motorboat from Harker's Island. We had a great time except for getting eaten alive by the huge mosquitoes. There were many ferries taken to the Outer Banks. Then we continued north to Virginia to see a handful of lights for the first time.

In late March 2004 we took a flight to Florida and began our twelve-day trip. We headed west to Alabama for the next day's private boat ride out to see Mobile Middle Bay light. Off to Mississippi and to Louisiana. While in Louisiana we went on a Swamp Tour to see some alligators and I even got to hold a baby one. We also took a short stroll on Bourbon Street and also went to the Audubon Aquarium of the Americas. We saw only a few on-shore lighthouses. We got back into Mississippi so we could get on the Ship Island Excursions boat. After the great day on the island, we headed east back to Florida. To see Cape St. George we chartered Captain Alex Crawford's boat and traveled a total of 22 miles. In 2005 it was destroyed by Hurricane Katrina. Out of Key West we got on our first seaplane and landed at Dry Tortugas 70 miles out to sea with a fly over of Loggerhead Key. After seeing the lighthouse and the fort, Seaplanes of Key West provided us with snorkel gear. It was like a comedy act when I was putting on the fins and then trying to breathe under water. The following day we took the Combo Pack-Max Access & the Cape Canaveral Then & Now bus tour, the only way, to see the lighthouse. We then traveled back to the west side of Florida to get on a ferry to Egmont Key. We had a great time here! We saw a surprisingly fast gopher tortoise, many palm trees and cool water to float in for hours.

For our early spring vacation in 2005 we visited Texas and Louisiana for six days. Two thirds of the lighthouses were easy to get to while the rest needed motor boats. At the Halfmoon Reef lighthouse, we were given a beautiful postcard. The lighthouse and grounds were covered in snow. It snows extremely rarely that far south. To see the Matagorda Island lighthouse, a man nicknamed "Pickles" took us out eleven miles on his fifteen-foot boat. We were then driven right up to the light. We even saw some wild turkeys and bottle-nose dolphins. Next, we got on a ferry to get to Aransas Pass and then a motor boat to get us closer to the lighthouse. Then we went all the way down to the Texas-Mexican border. Back to New Jersey to regroup. We had only two days of nice blue skies so we just took a quick trip down to Virginia. Then we went to Solomons, Maryland to have the Calvert Marine Museum shuttled us by van to the Cove Point Lighthouse. We took our shots while the sweat poured off us in buckets.

22

# Maryland and Washington, DC

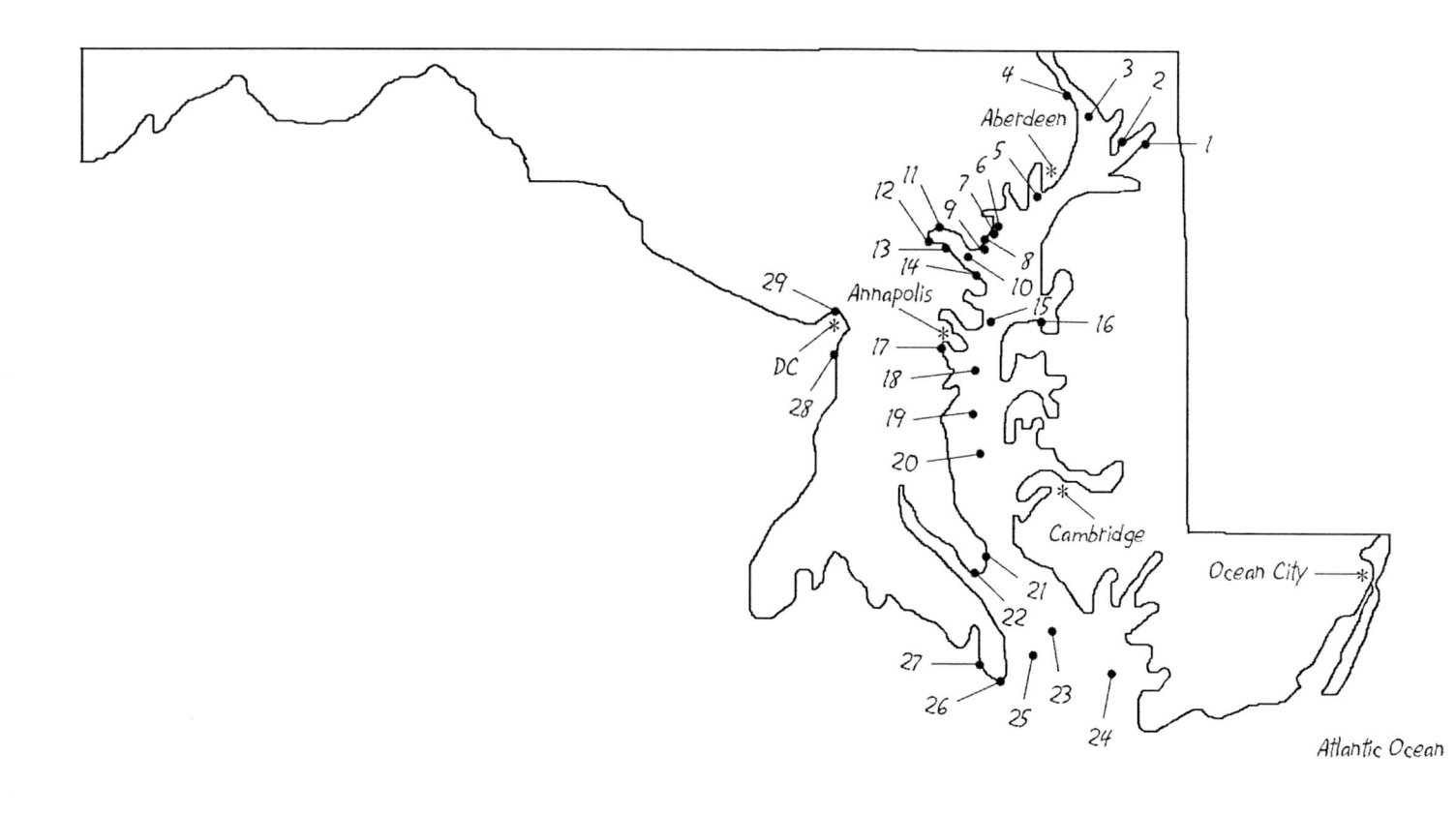

15.   Taken on 9-25-02

22.   Taken on 4-24-02

11.   Taken on 4-26-02

# Maryland and Washington, DC

1. 🚗 Bethel Bridge
2. 🚶 e Turkey Point
3. ⛴ Fishing Battery
4. 🚗 Concord Point
5. ⛴ Poole's Island
6. 🚗 Craighill Channel Lower Rear Range
7. ⛴ Craighill Channel Lower Front Range
8. 🚗 Craighill Channel Upper Rear Range
9. 🚗 Craighill Channel Upper Front Range
10. ⛴ Fort Carroll
11. 🚗 Seven Foot Knoll
12. 🚗 Lightship Chesapeake/LV-116/WAL-538
13. 🚗 Lazaretto Point
14. ⛴ Baltimore Harbor
15. ⛴ Sandy Point Shoal
16. 🚗 Hooper Strait
17. 🚗 Chesapeake Bay Lighthouse B&B
18. ⛴ Bloody Point Bar/The Coffee Pot
19. ⛴ Thomas Point Shoal
20. ⛴ Sharp's Island
21. 🚗 Cove Point
22. 🚗 Drum Point
23. ⛴ Hooper Island
24. ⛴ Point No Point
25. ⛴ Solomon's Lump
26. 🚗 Point Lookout
27. 🚗 Piney Point
28. 🚶 e Fort Washington
29. 🚶 e Jones Point

6. Taken on 9-25-02

14. Taken on 9-25-02

27. Taken on 3-22-05

# Virginia

1. 🚶 e  Assateague
2. ⛵  Cape Charles/Smith Island
3. 🚗  Old Cape Henry
4. 🚗  New Cape Henry
5. 🚗  Lightship Portsmouth/LV-101/WAL-524
6. ⛵  Newport News Middle Ground
7. 🚗  Old Point Comfort
8. ⛵  Thimble Shoal
9. ⛵  New Point Comfort
10. 🚗  Stingray Point Replica
11. ⛵  Wolf Trap
12. ⛵  Smith Point

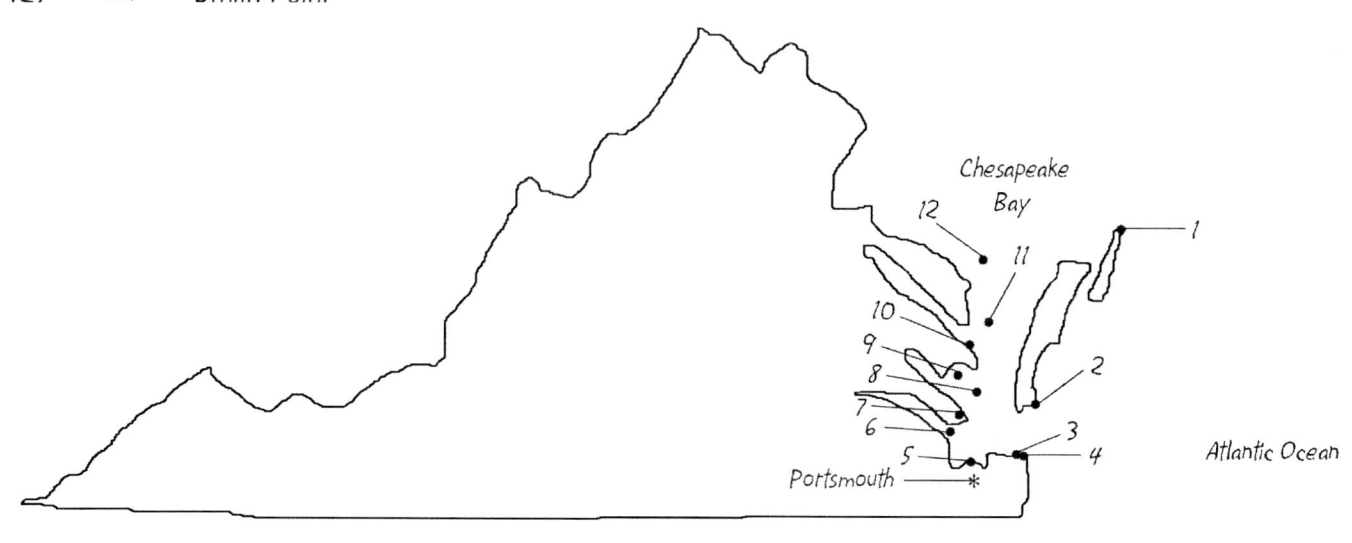

1. Taken on 4-17-03
4. Taken on 4-17-03 
7. Taken on 3-22-05

# North Carolina

1. 🚗 Currituck Beach/Whalehead
2. 🚗 Roanoke River
3. 🚗 Roanoke River Replica
4. 🚗 Roanoke Marshes Replica
5. 🚗 Bodie Island
6. 🚢 🚗 Cape Hatteras
7. ⛵ Diamond Shoals
8. 🚢 🚗 Ocracoke Island
9. ⛵ Cape Lookout
10. 🚢 🚶 e Bald Head/Old Baldy
11. 🚢 Price's Creek Front Range
12. 🚗 Oak Island

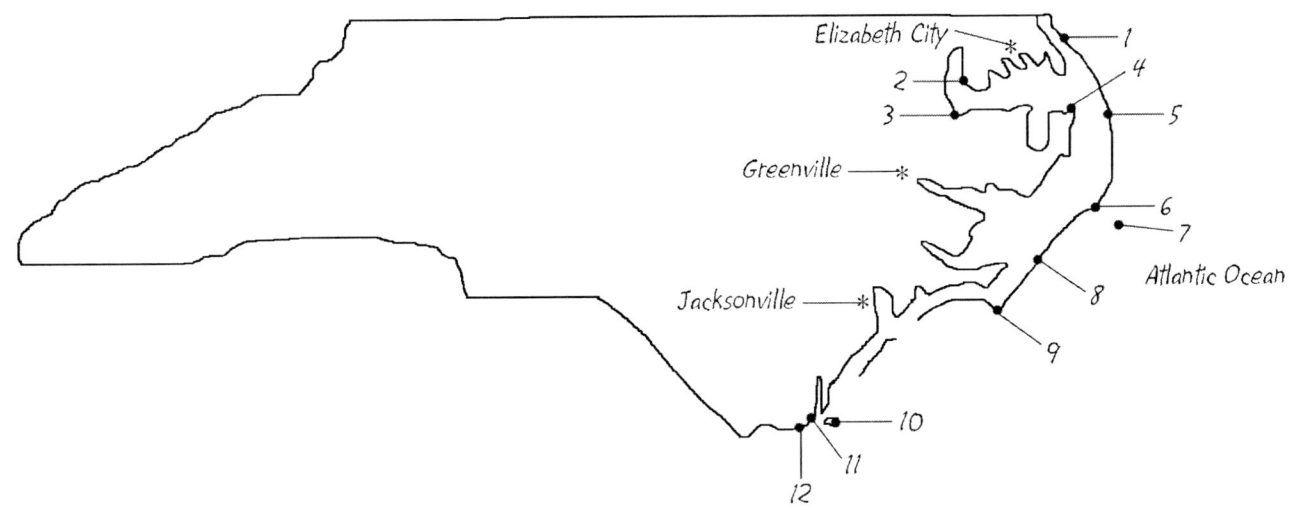

5. Taken on 4-15-03

10. Taken on 4-14-03

8. Taken on 4-15-03

# South Carolina

1. ⛵ Georgetown/North Island
2. ⛵ New Cape Romain
3. ⛵ Old Cape Romain
4. 🚗 Sullivan's Island/New Charleston
5. 🚶 e Morris Island/Old Charleston Harbor
6. 🚗 Hunting Island
7. 🚗 Old Hilton Head/Hilton Head Rear Range
8. 🚗 Harbor Town/Sea Pines
9. ⛵🚶 Haig Point Rear Range/Daufuskie Island
10. 🚢🚶 Bloody Point Rear Range

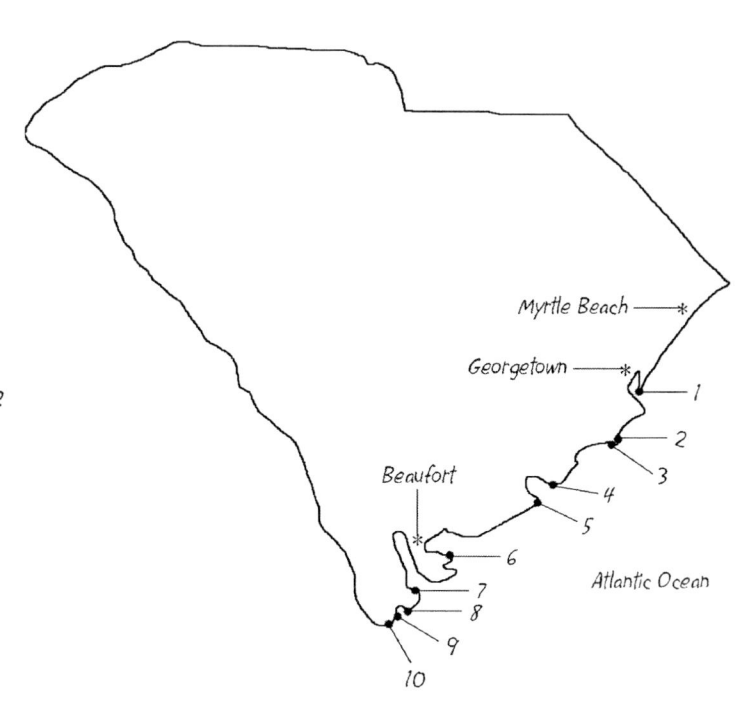

8. Taken on 4-12-03

6. Taken on 4-13-03

5. Taken on 4-13-03

# Georgia

1. 🚗 Tybee Island
2. 🚗 Cockspur Island
3. 🚗 Savannah Harbor Rear Range
4. ⛵ Sapelo Island
5. ⛵ Sapelo Island Front Range
6. 🚗 St. Simon's Island
7. ⛵ Little Cumberland Island

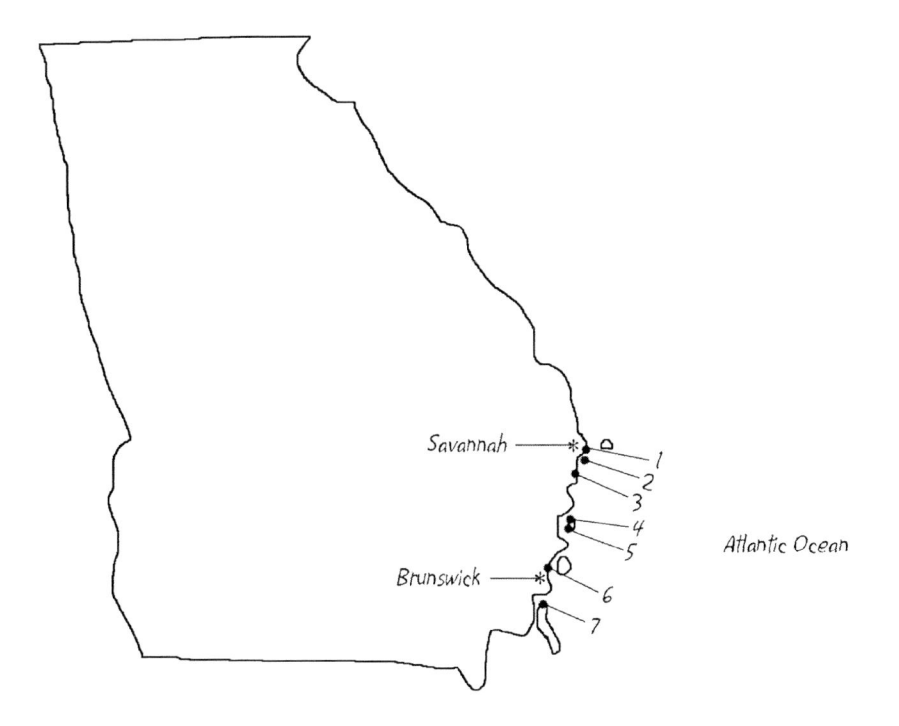

Savannah
Brunswick
Atlantic Ocean

1. Taken on 4-12-03
2. Taken on 4-12-03 
6. Taken on 4-12-03

# Florida

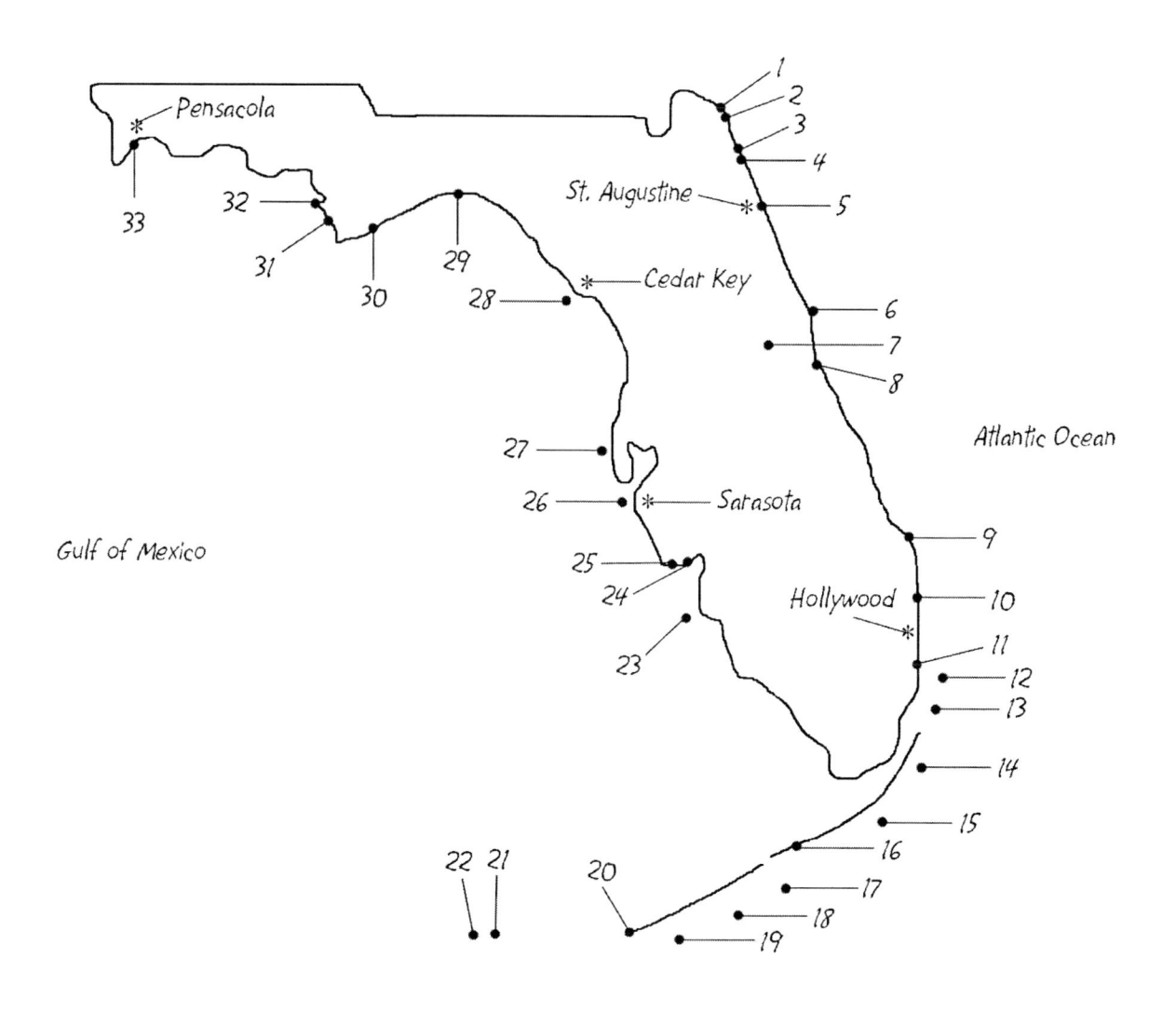

8.   Taken on 4-1-04

11.   Taken on 3-31-04

6.   Taken on 4-11-03

# Florida

1. 🚗 Amelia Island
2. 🚗 Amelia Island Replica
3. 🚗 St. John's Lightstation
4. 🚗 Mayport/St. John's River
5. 🚗 St. Augustine
6. 🚗 Ponce Inlet
7. 🚗 Mount Dora
8. 🚗 Cape Canaveral/Port Canaveral
9. 🚗 Jupiter Inlet
10. 🚗 Hillsborough Inlet
11. 🚗 Cape Florida
12. ⛵ Boca Chita
13. ⛵ Fowey Rocks
14. ⛵ Carysfort Reef
15. ⛵ Alligator Reef
16. 🚗 Faro Blanco
17. ⛵ Sombrero Key
18. ⛵ American Shoals
19. ⛵ Sand Key
20. 🚗 Key West/Whitehead's Point
21. ✈ Tortugas Harbor/Fort Jefferson/Garden Key
22. ✈ Loggerhead Key/Dry Tortugas
23. 🚗 Sanibel Island
24. 🚗 Boca Grande/Old Port Boca Grande/Gasparilla Island
25. 🚗 Boca Grande Entrance Rear Range/Gasparilla R. Range
26. ⛵ Egmont Key
27. ⛵ Anclote Key
28. ⛵ Cedar Keys/Seahorse Key
29. 🚗 St. Marks Rear Range
30. 🚗 Crooked River
31. 🚗 Cape San Blas
32. 🚗 St. Joseph Bay/St. Joseph Point
33. 🚗 Pensacola

10. Taken on 3-31-04

21. Taken on 3-30-04

26. Taken on 4-2-04

# Alabama

1. ⛵ Mobile Middle Bay/Middle Bay
2. 🚗 Mobile Point Rear Range
3. ⛵ Sand Island
4. 🚗 Norwegian Light Beacon

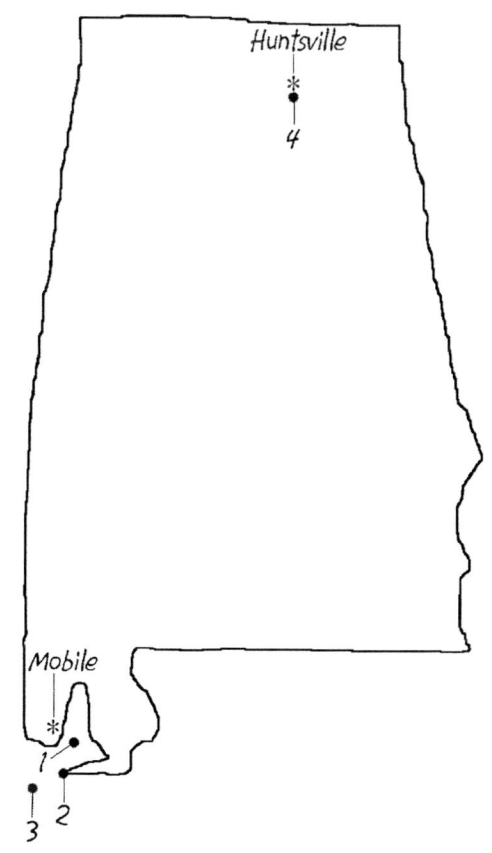

Gulf of Mexico

1. Taken on 3-24-04

# Mississippi

1. 🚗 Chickasawhay River
2. 🚗 Biloxi
3. 🚗 Merchant Marine Sailors Monument
4. ⛵ Ship Island Rear Range

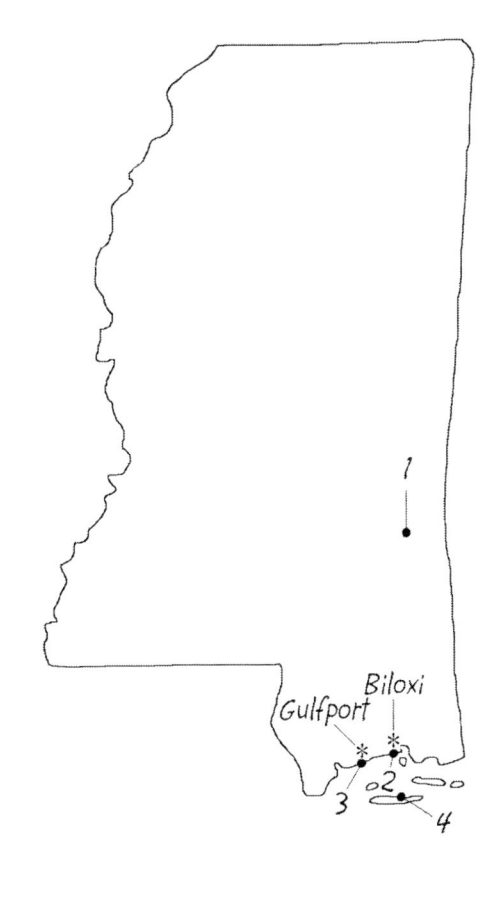

Gulf of Mexico

4. Taken on 3-27-04

2. Taken on 3-24-04

3. Taken on 3-27-04

# Louisiana

32

Madisonville

3  2  *  1

Berwick

4  *  5

New Orleans

13

12

11

Gulf of Mexico

8
9
10

6
7

5.   Taken on 3-26-04     4.   Taken on 3-26-04     2.   Taken on 3-24-04

## Louisiana

1. 🚗 West Rigolets
2. 🚗 Tchefuncte River Rear Range
3. ⛵ Pass Manchac
4. 🚗 New Canal
5. 🚗 Port Ponchartrain
6. ⛵ Pass A'L'Outre
7. ⛵ South Pass Rear Range/Gordon's Island
8. ⛵ Southwest Pass-old
9. ⛵ Southwest Pass-new
10. ⛵ Southwest Pass Entrance
11. ⛵ Ship Shoal
12. 🚗 Southwest Reef
13. 🚗 Sabine Pass

1. Taken on 3-26-04

12. Taken on 3-25-04

# Texas

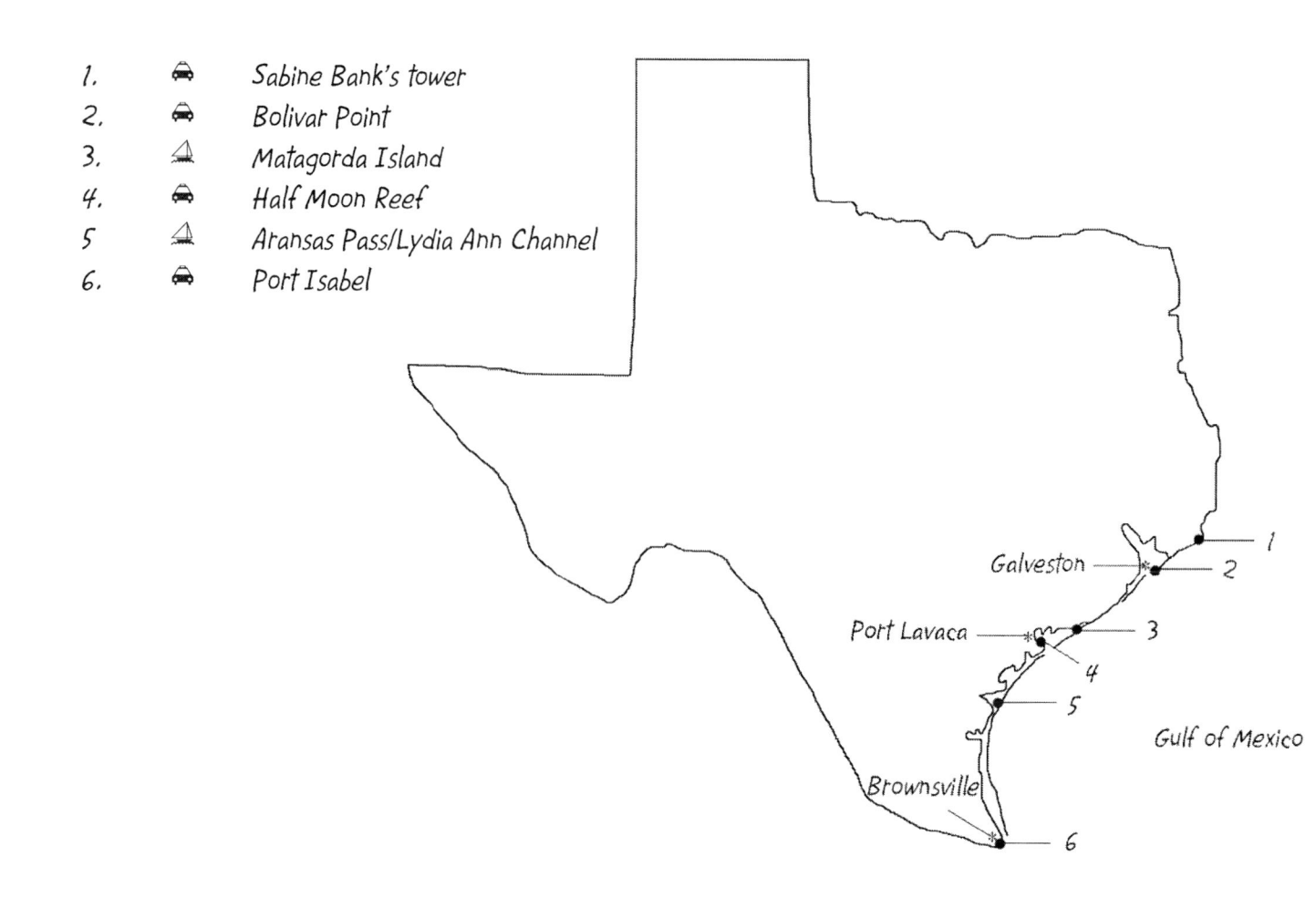

1. 🚗 Sabine Bank's tower
2. 🚗 Bolivar Point
3. ⛵ Matagorda Island
4. 🚗 Half Moon Reef
5. ⛵ Aransas Pass/Lydia Ann Channel
6. 🚗 Port Isabel

3. Taken on 3-17-05

4. Taken on 3-14-05

6. Taken on 3-17-05

# Vermont

1. 🚗 Windmill Point
2. 🚗 Isle La Motte
3. ⛵ Juniper Island
4. 🚗 Burlington North Breakwater
5. 🚗 Burlington South Breakwater
6. 🚗 Colchester Reef

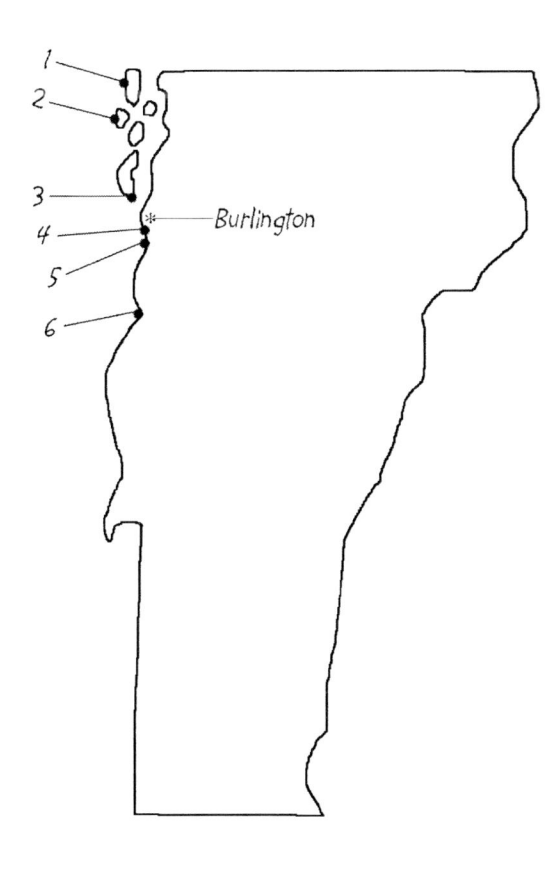

1. Taken on 10-3-03

6. Taken on 10-3-03

2. Taken on 10-3-03

# Upper New York

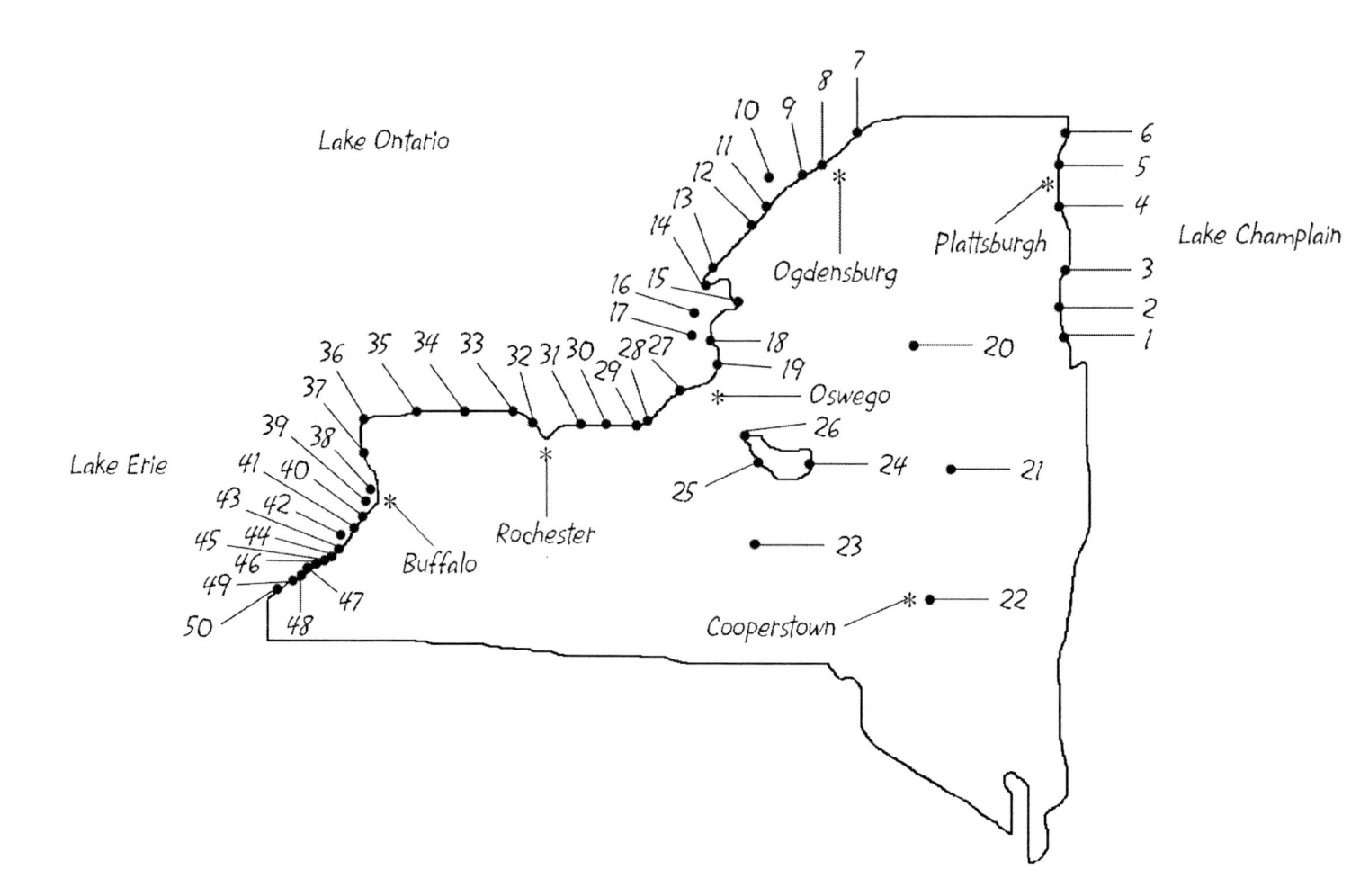

Lake Ontario

Lake Champlain

Plattsburgh

Ogdensburg

Lake Erie

Rochester

Oswego

Buffalo

Cooperstown

40.   Taken on 9-22-06

19.   Taken on 9-20-06

14.   Taken on 9-21-06

## Upper New York

1. 🚗 Crown Point
2. 🚗 Barbers Point
3. ⛵ Split Rock Point
4. ⛵ Bluff Point/Valcour Island
5. 🚶 e Cumberland Head
6. 🚗 Point Au Roche
7. 🚗 Ogdensburg Harbor
8. 🚗 Crossover Island
9. ⛵ Sisters Island/Three Sisters Island
10. 🚗 Sunken Rock
11. 🚗 Soldier's Memorial
12. ⛵ Rock Island
13. 🚗 Cape Vincent Breakwater
14. 🚗 Tibbetts Point
15. ⛵ Horse Island/Sacketts Harbor
16. ⛵ East Charity Shoal
17. ⛵ Galloo Island
18. 🚗 Stony Point
19. 🚗 Selkirk/Salmon River
20. 🚗 Shoal Point
21. 🚗 Erie Canal
22. 🚗 Cooperstown Marina
23. 🚗 Myers Point
24. 🚗 Verona Beach/Sylvan Beach/Barge Canal
25. 🚗 Frenchman's Island
26. 🚗 Brewerton Rear Range
27. 🚗 Oswego West Pierhead
28. 🚗 Sodus Bay Pierhead/Sodus Outer
29. 🚗 Old Sodus Point/Big Sodus Point
30. 🚗 Irondequoit Bay West Pier
31. 🚗 Charlotte-Genessee/Port of Genessee
32. 🚶 e Rochester Harbor
33. 🚗 Braddock Point
34. 🚗 Thirty Mile Point
35. 🚗 Olcott Replica
36. 🚗 Old Fort Niagara
37. 🚗 Grand Island Old Front Range/Niagara River Old F.R.
38. ⛵ Horseshoe Reef
39. ⛵ Buffalo Intake Crib

8. Taken on 9-21-06

13. Taken on 9-21-06

37. Taken on 9-22-06

## Upper New York continued

40. 🚶 e   Old Buffalo Main/Chinaman's
41. 🚶 e   Buffalo Old Bottle Breakwater/Buffalo North Breakwater
42. ⛵   Buffalo Breakwater/Buffalo Outer Breakwater
43. ⛵   South Buffalo South Side
44. 🚗   Sturgeon Point
45. 🚗   Dunkirk/Fort Gratiot
46. 🚗   Grand Island Rear Range
47. 🚗   South Buffalo North Side/South Buffalo Bottle
48. 🚗   Old Dunkirk Pierhead
49. 🚗   Dunkirk Pierhead/Dunkirk Modern
50. 🚗   Barcelona

50. Taken on 9-28-06

# Pennsylvania

1. 🚗 Erie Land/Old Presque Isle
2. 🚗 Erie Pierhead/Erie Harbor North Pier
3. 🚗 Presque Isle
4. 🚗 Erie Yacht Club Breakwater
5. 🚗 Schuylkill River/Turtle Rock

Lake Erie

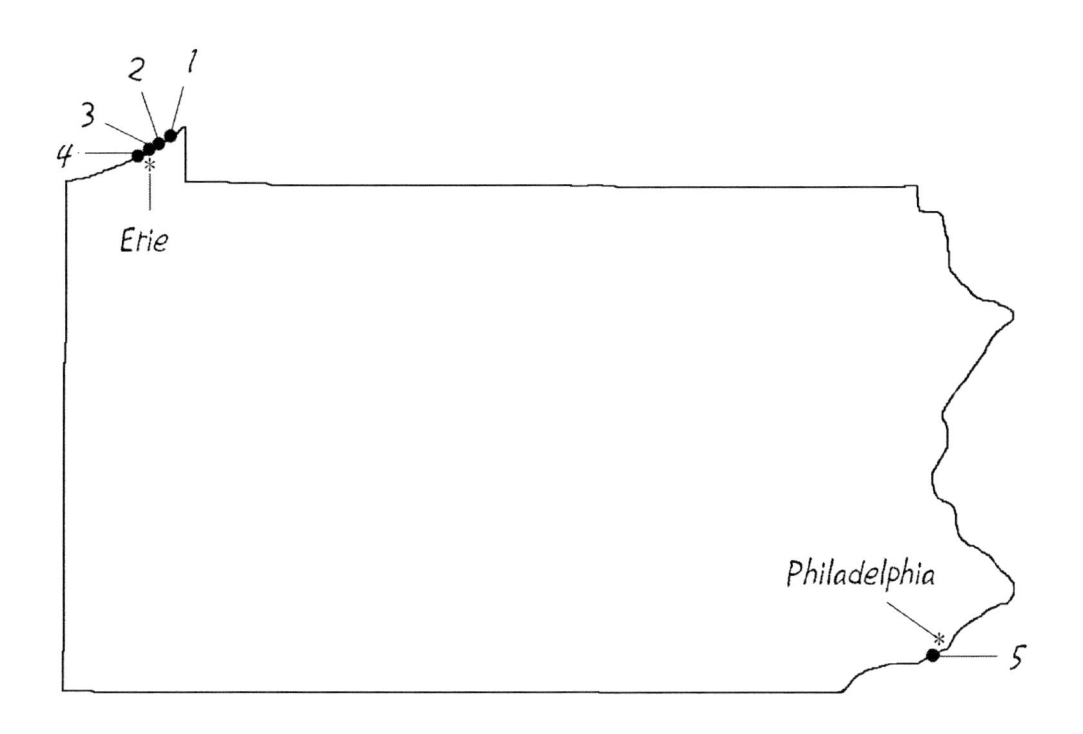

Erie

Philadelphia

1. Taken on 9-29-06

5. Taken on 4-27-02

2. Taken on 9-27-06

# Ohio

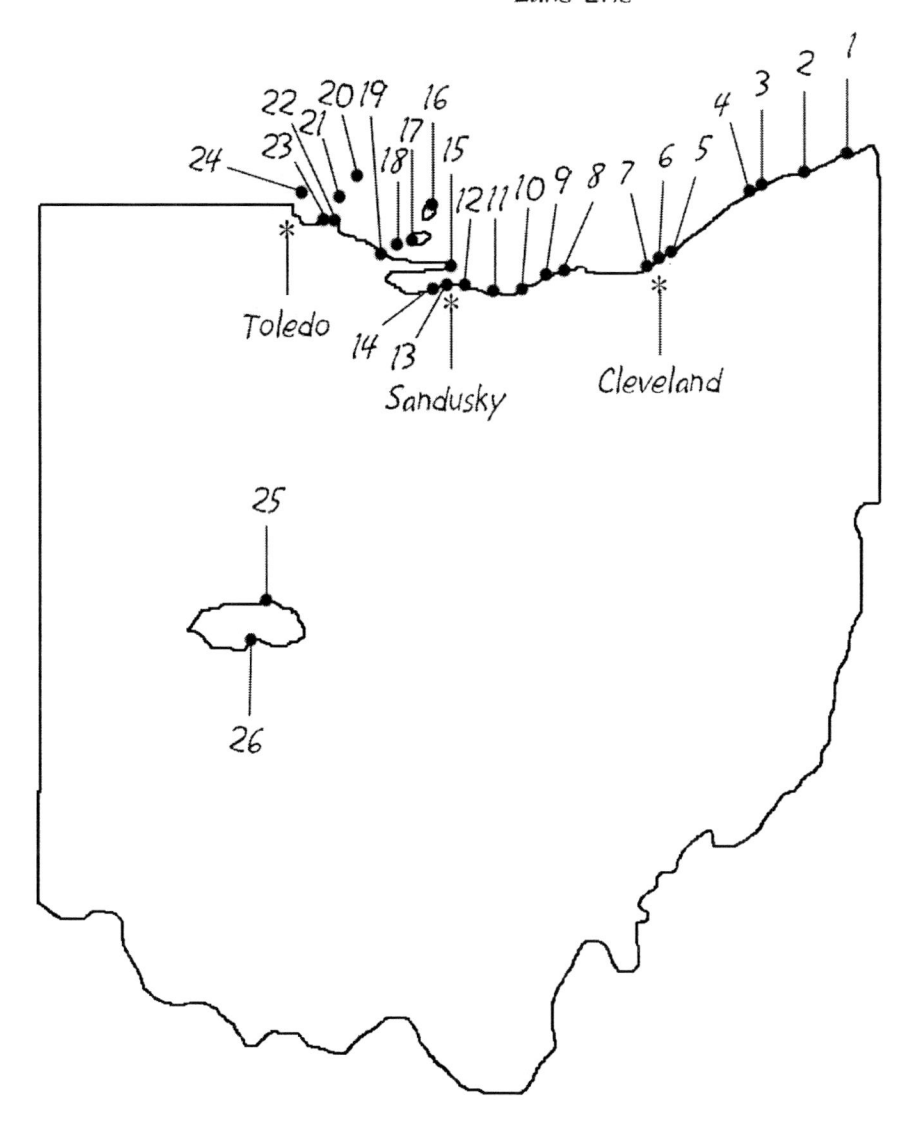

40

Lake Erie

Toledo
Sandusky
Cleveland

15. Taken on 9-26-06     8. Taken on 9-24-06     12. Taken on 9-26-06

# Ohio

1. 🚗 Conneaut Harbor West Breakwater
2. 🚶 m Ashtabula Harbor Entrance
3. 🚗 Fairport Harbor Old Main/Grand River
4. 🚶 m Fairport Harbor West Breakwater
5. ⛵ Cleveland East Entrance
6. 🚗 Cleveland Harbor East Pierhead
7. 🚗 Cleveland West Breakwater
8. 🚗 Lorain West Breakwater/Jewel of the Port
9. 🚗 Lorain East Breakwater
10. 🚗 Vermilion Replica
11. 🚶 e Huron Harbor Pierhead
12. 🚗 Cedar Point
13. ⛵ Sandusky Harbor Pierhead
14. 🚗 Point Retreat
15. 🚗 Marblehead/Sandusky Bay
16. ⛴ Perry's International Peace Memorial
17. ⛴ 🚶 e South Bass Island
18. ⛵ Green Island
19. 🚗 Old Port Clinton
20. ⛵ West Sister Island
21. ⛵ Turtle Island
22. 🚗 Manhattan Rear Range
23. 🚗 Manhattan Front Range
24. ⛵ Toledo Harbor
25. 🚗 Grand Lake St. Mary
26. 🚗 Northwood

3. Taken on 9-27-06

10. Taken on 9-24-06

# Lower Michigan

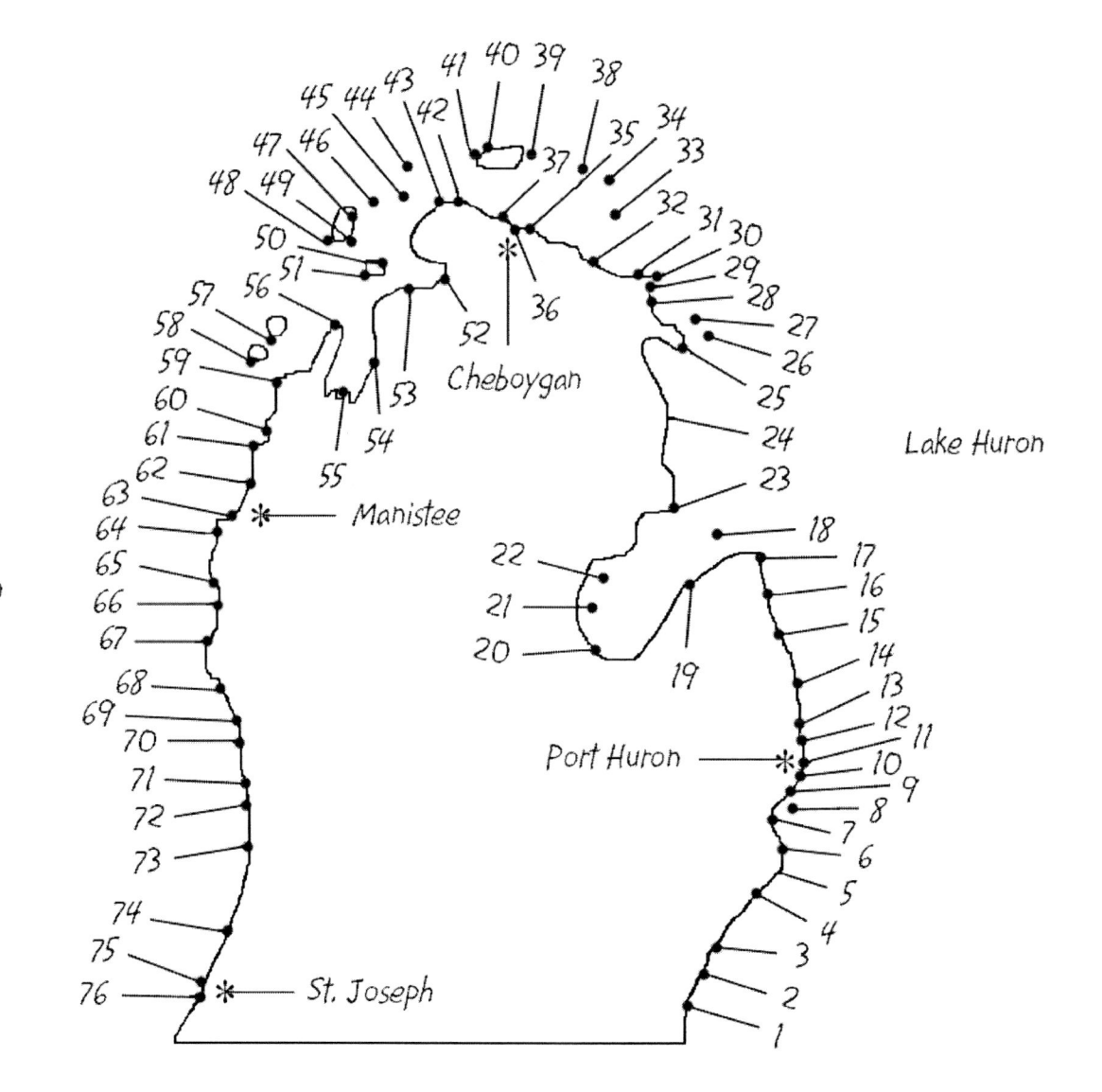

42

Cheboygan

Lake Huron

Manistee

Lake Michigan

Port Huron

St. Joseph

67.  Taken on 10-3-01

73.  Taken on 10-1-05

42.  Taken on 9-27-05

## Lower Michigan

1. 🚗 Detroit River
2. ⛴ Grosse Ile North Channel Front Range
3. 🚗 Mariners Memorial
4. 🚗 William Livingston Memorial
5. 🚗 Windmill Point
6. ⛴ Lake St. Clair
7. 🚗 Colony Tower
8. ⛴ Harsen's Island Range
9. 🚢🚗 St. Clair Flats Old Channel Front Range
10. 🚢🚗 St. Clair Flats Old Channel Rear Range
11. 🚗 Peche Island Old Rear Range
12. 🚗 Lightship Huron/Old B.O./LV-103/WAL-526
13. 🚗 Fort Gratiot
14. 🚗 Port Sanilac
15. 🚗 White Rock
16. ⛴ Harbor Beach/Sand Beach
17. 🚗 Point Aux Barques
18. ⛴ Port Austin Reef
19. 🚗 Caseville/Pigeon River
20. ⛴ Saginaw River Rear Range
21. ⛴ Gravelly Shoal
22. ⛴ Charity Island
23. 🚗 Tawas Point/Ottawa
24. 🚗 Sturgeon Point
25. 🚗 Alpena
26. ⛴ Thunder Bay Island
27. ⛴ Middle Island
28. 🚗 Presque Isle Harbor Old Front Range
29. 🚗 Presque Isle Harbor Old Rear Range
30. 🚗 Old Presque Isle
31. 🚗 Presque Isle/New Presque Island
32. 🚗 Forty Mile Point
33. ⛴ Poe Reef
34. ⛴ Spectacle Reef
35. 🚗 Cheboygan River Front Range
36. 🚗 Cheboygan Crib
37. 🚗 Cheboygan Crib Breakwater
38. ⛴ Fourteen Foot Shoal
39. ⛴ Bois Blanc Island

4. Taken on 9-17-01

17. Taken on 9-29-05

33. Taken on 9-27-05

## Lower Michigan continued

40. ⛵ Round Island
41. ⛵ Round Island Passage
42. 🚗 Old Mackinac Point
43. 🚗 McGulpin Point
44. ⛵ White Shoal
45. ⛵ Waugoshance
46. ⛵ Gray's Reef
47. 🚢🚗 Beaver Island Harbor/St. James Harbor
48. 🚢🚗 Beaver Island/Beaver Head
49. ⛵ Skillagalee/Ile Aux Galets
50. ✈ Old South Fox Island
51. ✈ South Fox Island
52. ⛵ Little Traverse/Harbor Point
53. 🚗 Petosky Pierhead
54. 🚗 Charlevoix South Pierhead
55. 🚗 Old Mission Point
56. 🚗 Grand Traverse/Cats Head Point
57. 🚢 North Manitou Island Shoal
58. 🚢 🚶 e South Manitou Island
59. 🚗 Robert H. Manning Memorial
60. 🚗 Point Betsie
61. 🚗 Frankfort North Breakwater/Frankfort Pier
62. 🚗 Manistee North Pierhead
63. 🚶 m Big Sable Point/Grand Point Au Sable
64. 🚗 Ludington North Breakwater
65. 🚗 Pentwater North Pierhead
66. 🚗 Pentwater South Pierhead
67. 🚗 Little Sable Point
68. 🚗 White River Main
69. 🚗 Muskegon Harbor Breakwater
70. 🚗 Muskegon Harbor South Pierhead
71. 🚶 e Grand Haven South Pierhead Inner
72. 🚶 e Grand Haven South Pierhead Entrance Outer
73. 🚗 Holland Harbor South Pierhead/Big Red
74. 🚶 e South Haven Harbor South Pierhead
75. 🚗 St. Joseph North Pier Inner
76. 🚗 St. Joseph North Pier Outer

40. Taken on 9-27-05

63. Taken on 10-2-05

71. Taken on 10-1-05

## Our Great Lake Hunts

For six days in June 2001 we decided to head northwest and begin our Great Lake lighthouse journey. We headed north to Lake Champlain, then to the lakes. We went through New York, of course stopping at Niagara Falls, Pennsylvania, and Ohio. We often have to rely on local knowledge. Sometimes it's very helpful and sometimes we ask the wrong people. We often hear, "We have a lighthouse around here?" This has happened many times, especially while in Vermont.

We had three weeks in late September and early October 2001 for our vacation. We went to Michigan, Indiana, Illinois, Wisconsin, Michigan's Upper Peninsula and Minnesota only five days after the attack on our country. We saw many flags waving during our travels and we are proud to be Americans. This was "our world record" trip. In twenty days we saw 158 lighthouses in these five states. Wow! The state of Michigan has the most lighthouses of all the US states.

We've been very busy in the summer of 2005 working hard on this, our first book. It's been taking up all of our spare time. We get started right away when we come home from work. On our days off and of course Sunday we work on it non-stop. Off on another trip, this time flying to Wisconsin and Michigan for fifteen days in late September and early October 2005. The temperature in New Jersey has been in the mid-80's and humid. It should be cooler in Great Lakes and we can't wait! We took the 140-mile Apostle Island Cruise on the Island Princess out of Bayfield, Wisconsin to see six lights. Out of Mackinaw City, Michigan we loaded onto the Shepler's Lighthouse Cruise boat to travel forty miles in three hours to see eight lighthouses. We got significantly closer to many of the eastern off-shore lights. The following day was supposed to be the westbound trip but it was canceled due to rough seas.

We have walked on many breakwaters, beaches and trails to get close to the lighthouses. The beautiful red lighthouses on the west side of Lower Michigan were just fantastic! We've waited a long time for these perfect shots. One night we were able to see the last few seconds of a beautiful sunset while just getting to Little Sable Light. We wanted to get there for the late afternoon sun but we were doing other lighthouses. The next morning we got some great shots of the light just as the sun was coming up over the trees. There were many high sand dunes there, and it was tiresome to walk. A few lighthouses later we did the 3-½ mile round trip walk to the Big Sable lighthouse again. The lighthouse has a bus that will take you there only a few days out of the year. We are never there during the summer months to take advantage of it. We worked our way back to Wisconsin and to the Door County Peninsula for my 40th birthday on Thursday, October 6th.

Most lights on the breakwaters look better from a beach or from the adjacent breakwater. That way if it's windy the choppy water smashes into the breakwater and the water shoots up! We love when that happens.

By the end of this trip we had seen a grand total of 1,052 lighthouses in the United States and Canada. This is a great accomplishment for us and we are still not finished. There are still many more lighthouses to see throughout the world. It all begins by visiting your first lighthouse.

*How many will you visit?*

# Upper Michigan

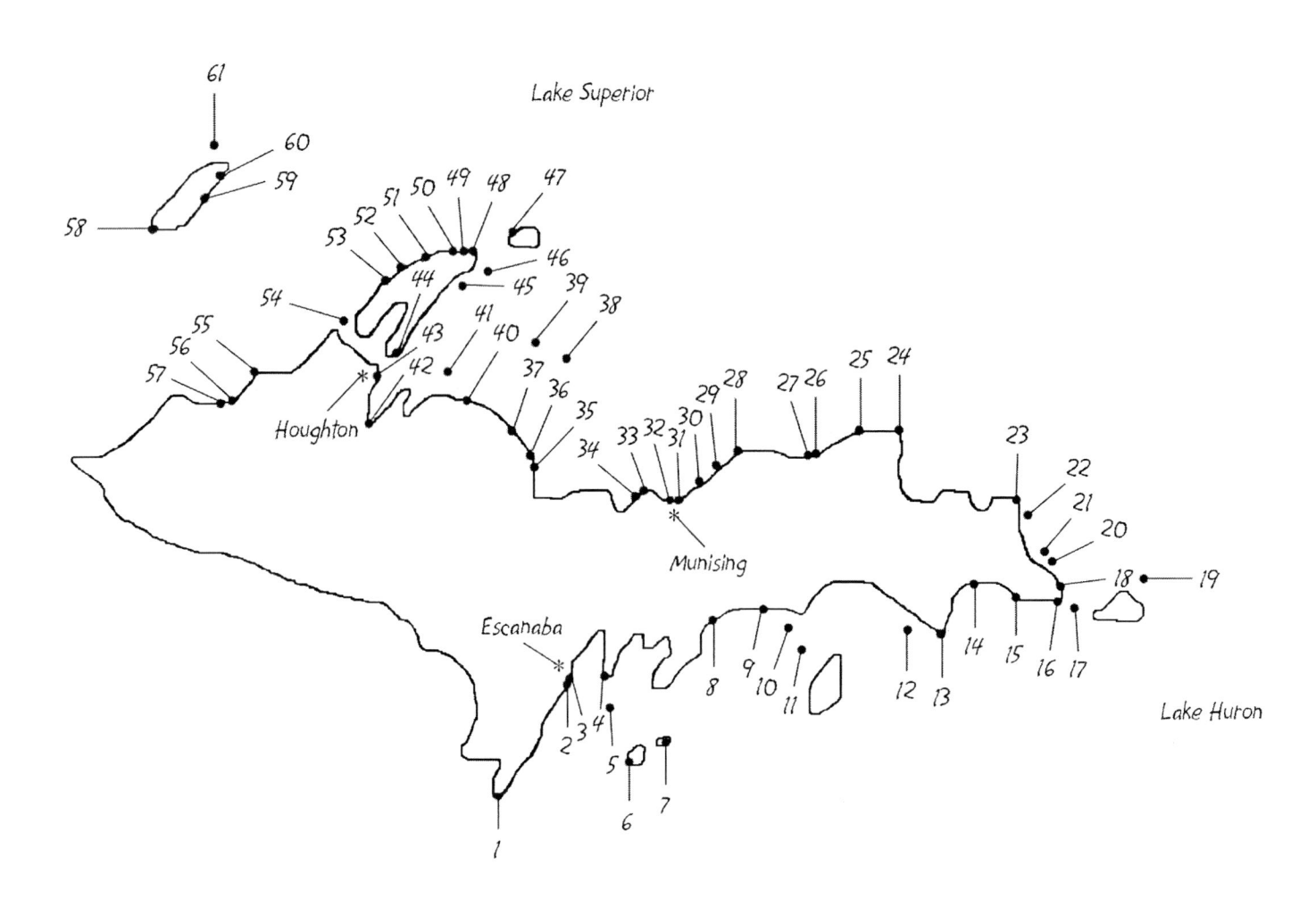

Lake Superior

Houghton

Munising

Escanaba

Lake Huron

Lake Michigan

25.     Taken on 10-4-05

40.     Taken on 9-26-01

3.     Taken on 10-5-05

# Upper Michigan

1. 🚗 Menominee North Pierhead
2. 🚗 Escanaba Harbor
3. 🚗 Escanaba Sand Point
4. 🚗 Peninsula Point
5. ⛵ Minneapolis Shoal
6. ⛵ St. Martin Island
7. ⛵ Poverty Island
8. 🚗 Manistique East Breakwater
9. 🚗 Seul Choix Point
10. ⛵ Squaw Island
11. ⛵ Lansing Shoal
12. ⛵ St. Helena Island
13. 🚗 St. Ignace Fake
14. ⛵ Martin Reef
15. 🚗 Les Cheneaux Range
16. 🚗 DeTour Village Range
17. ⛵ DeTour Reef
18. 🚗 Frying Pan Island
19. ⛵ Pipe Island
20. ⛵ Round Island/St. Mary's
21. 🚢 🚗 Middle Neebish Front Range
22. ⛵ Cedar Point Rear Range
23. 🚗 Point Iroquois
24. 🚗 Whitefish Point
25. 🚗 Crisp Point
26. 🚗 Grand Marais Harbor Front Range
27. 🚗 Grand Marais Harbor Rear Range
28. 🚶 m Au Sable Point
29. 🚢 🚶 m Grand Island Old North Point
30. ⛵ Grand Island East Channel
31. 🚗 Munising Front Range
32. 🚗 Munising Rear Range
33. 🚗 Grand Island Harbor Front Range/End of the Road F.R.
34. 🚗 Grand Island Harbor Rear Range/End of the Road R.R.
35. 🚗 Marquette Harbor
36. 🚗 Marquette Lower Harbor
37. 🚗 Presque Isle Harbor Breakwater
38. ⛵ Granite Island
39. ⛵ Stannard Rock

1. Taken on 10-5-05

24. Taken on 9-22-01

37. Taken on 9-26-05

## Upper Michigan continued

40. 🚗 Big Bay Point
41. ⛴ Huron Island
42. 🚗 Sand Point
43. 🚶 e Portage River Lower Entrance/Keweenaw W. L. Entrance
44. 🚗 Portage River/Jacobsville
45. 🚗 Bete Grise/Mendota
46. ⛴ Gull Rock
47. ⛴ Manitou Island
48. 🚗 Copper Harbor Rear Range
49. 🚗 Copper Harbor Front Range
50. 🚢 Copper Harbor
51. 🚗 Eagle Harbor
52. 🚗 Eagle River
53. 🚗 Sand Hills/Five Mile Point
54. 🚗 Keweenau Waterway Upper Entrance/Portage Lake S. Canal
55. ⛴ Fourteen Mile Point
56. 🚗 Ontonogon
57. 🚗 Ontonogon West Pierhead
58. ⛴ Rock of Ages
59. ⛴ Isle Royale/Menagerie Island
60. ⛴ Rock Harbor
61. ⛴ Passage Island

42. Taken on 9-26-05

54. Taken on 9-25-01

# Indiana

1. 🚗 Michigan City East Pier
2. 🚗 Michigan City East Breakwater
3. 🚗 Old Michigan City/Old Lighthouse Museum
4. 🚗 The Lighthouse Place Information Center
5. ⛵ Gary Breakwater
6. ⛵ Buffington Harbor Breakwater
7. ⛵ Indiana Harbor East Breakwater

3. Taken on 9-25-06

1. Taken on 9-25-06

2. Taken on 9-25-06

# Illinois

1. ⛵ Calumet Harbor Breakwater South End
2. 🚗 Chicago Harbor Southeast Guide Wall
3. 🚗 Chicago Harbor
4. 🚗 Grosse Point
5. 🚗 Waukegan Harbor/Little Fort

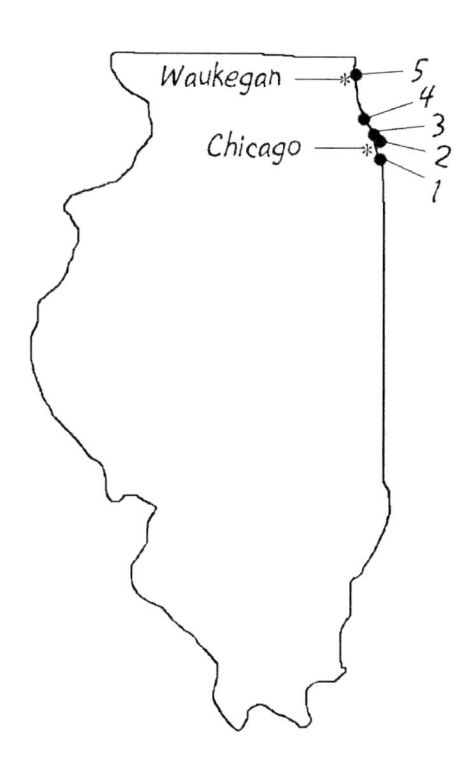

Waukegan
Chicago
Lake Michigan

2. Taken on 9-25-06

3. Taken on 9-25-06

5. Taken on 9-25-06

## Our Pacific Coast Hunts

In June 2002 we decided to head west to California and Oregon to begin our West Coast lighthouse vacation. One day we walked seven miles on a beach to an abandoned lighthouse. This proved to be an exhausting four-hour adventure. In June 2003 we traveled west again but this time to Washington. One ferry ride was to Whidbey Island to see a beautiful lighthouse. We traveled the coast and especially enjoyed the most northwestern tip of the US because of it's beautiful cliffs with crashing waves.

In July 2004, a 14-day trip to the Hawaiian Islands was both pleasure and business. Just like all the other trips, this took months to prepare. The planning of the flights from home and then the island hopping were a challenge. The most difficult lighthouse to plan was near the Leper Colony in Kalaupapa on Molokai. We knew this trip, like most of the others, was going to be very rushed. Boy, were we ever right! In five days we traveled all around the islands of Maui, Molokai, The Big Island, and Kauai. The following week we spent on Oahu for a convention. Each island had its own character and uniqueness. We hiked to waterfalls, tidal pools, rainforests and lighthouses. We walked through rivers, over slippery roots and rocks, while going up and down a mountain in 86-degree temperatures.

We took a prop-plane from Kahului, Maui to Kalaupapa, Molokai. What a beautiful sight to see the island and its cliffs and mountains from the air! It was incredible! Once on the ground we went on a tour of Kalaupapa's Leper Colony with a member of Father Damien's group. We saw much beautiful scenery. Then we were driven up the hill to the lighthouse. The scenic flight back to Maui was exciting. One morning we saw the sunrise from the 9,740 foot summit of Haleakala. Next was The Big Island where we had arranged for Bill and Sandie Wong of ATV-Outfitters to take us to see a lighthouse. Later we went to the most southern spot in the whole United States to see a small lighthouse. Then off to Kauai, the island we loved the best. It was just beautiful! We then spent a week in Honolulu, Oahu for our Union Convention. We enjoyed a sunset buffet aboard a catamaran, and a luau on a beautiful beach while watching the sun go down. The palm trees were lovely. We enjoyed frolicking in the aqua-colored water. Before heading home we snorkeled and saw the remaining lighthouses of our Hawaiian adventure.

For three weeks in late spring 2005 we headed to the last frontier, Alaska. Coordinating the ten jets, six rental cars, five float or wheel planes, two ferries, two boats, two skiffs and a kayak was an extremely challenging task. Mostly every night we slept in a different city. It was incredible to view a sunset at midnight. We loved the beautiful hills and mountains that we got to see from the air, sea and land. It was fantastic to see the numerous variety of wildlife and sea life. Tommy's had a great 54th birthday and we saw a few humpback whales while heading towards a lighthouse. We loved the snow-covered mountains of British Columbia and the Yukon Territory. We photographed all the lighthouses in Alaska. Each one had its own thrilling story. The months of planning really paid off. This was a trip of a lifetime. One morning we had the chance to go on a glacier walk. The experience of flying over the wilderness was breathtaking. Our two-week trip in Alaska came to an end when our one-week in Washington began. Kayaking six miles to a lighthouse was new to the both of us. The private four-hour charter we took around the San Juan Islands was more pleasurable for us.

# Wisconsin

Lake Superior

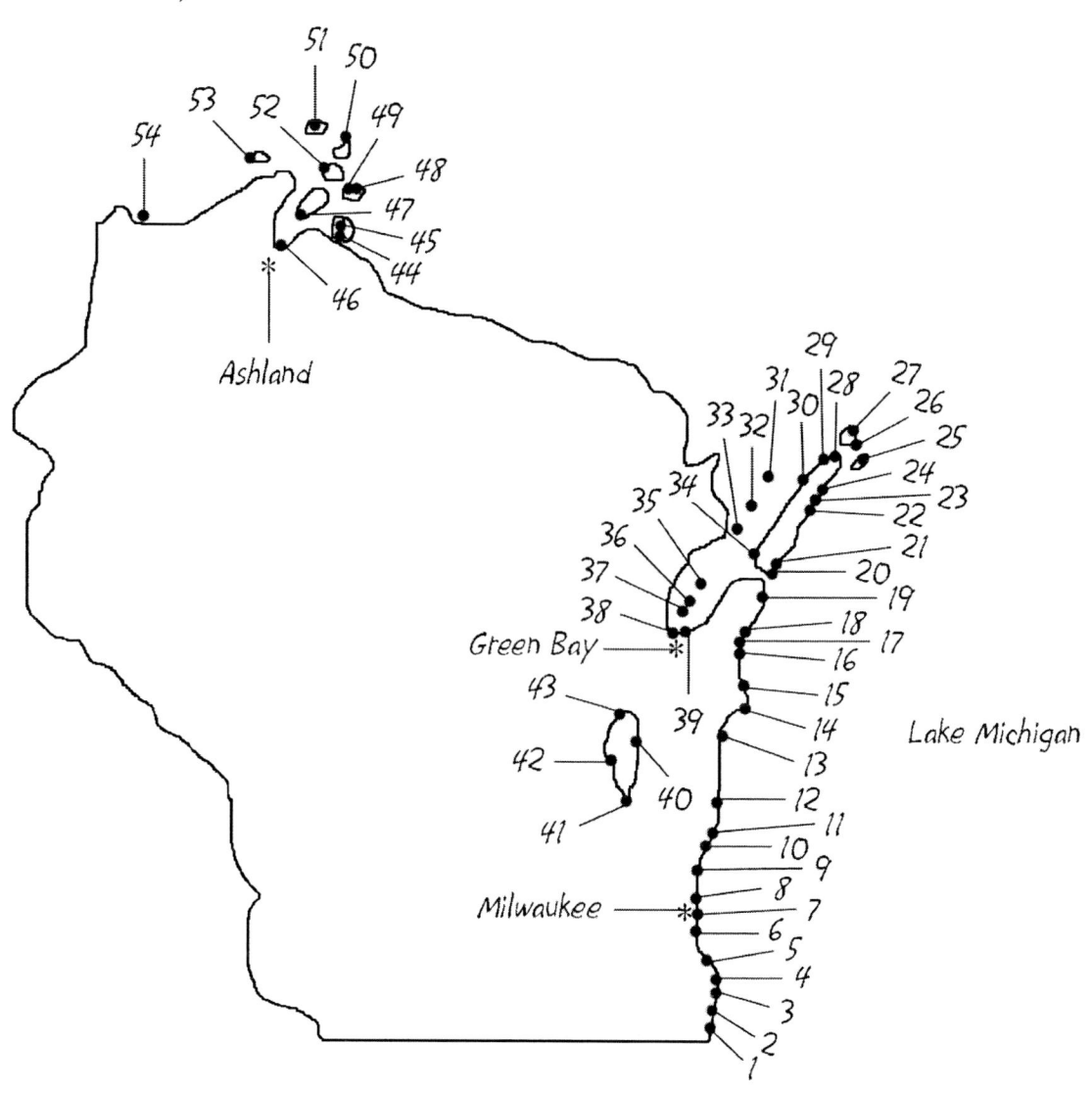

Ashland

Green Bay

Milwaukee

Lake Michigan

54.     Taken on 9-24-01

7.     Taken on 9-30-01

5.     Taken on 9-30-01

# Wisconsin

1. 🚗 Old Kenosha/Southport
2. 🚗 Kenosha Pierhead/Kenosha North Pier
3. 🚗 Racine South Breakwater
4. 🚗 Racine North Breakwater/Big Red
5. 🚗 Wind Point Racine
6. 🚶 e Milwaukee Breakwater
7. 🚶 e Milwaukee Pierhead
8. 🚗 North Point/Milwaukee
9. 🚗 Kevich
10. 🚗 Port Washington Breakwater
11. 🚗 Old Port Washington
12. 🚶 e Sheboygan Breakwater
13. 🚗 Manitowoc Breakwater
14. 🚗 Two Rivers North Pierhead
15. 🚶 e Rawley Point/Twin River Point
16. 🚗 Kewaunee South Pierhead
17. 🚗 Kewaunee Information Center
18. 🚗 The Lighthouse Shop
19. 🚗 Algoma Pierhead Front/Algoma North Pierhead
20. 🚶 e Sturgeon Bay Ship Canal North Pierhead
21. 🚶 e Sturgeon Bay Ship Canal
22. 🚗 Bailey's Harbor Front Range
23. 🚗 Bailey's Harbor Rear Range
24. 🚗 Old Bailey's Harbor
25. 🚗 Cana Island
26. ⛵ Pilot Island/Port des Morts
27. ⛵ Pottawatamie
28. 🚢 Plum Island Front Range
29. 🚢 Plum Island Rear Range
30. 🚗 Eagle Bluff
31. ⛵ Chamber's Island
32. ⛵ Green Island
33. ⛵ Peshtigo Reef
34. 🚗 Sherwood Point
35. ⛵ Green Bay Harbor Entrance
36. ⛵ Old Long Tail Point
37. ⛵ New Long Tail Point
38. 🚗 Grassy Island Front Range
39. 🚗 Grassy Island Rear Range

4. Taken on 9-30-01

21. Taken on 9-29-01

25. Taken on 10-6-05

## Wisconsin continued

40. 🚗 Pipe
41. 🚗 Fond du Lac
42. 🚗 Brays Point
43. 🚗 Kimberly Point
44. ⛵ Chequamegon Point
45. ⛵ Chequamegon Point Modern
46. 🚗 Ashland Breakwater
47. ⛵ La Pointe/Long Island
48. ⛵ Michigan Island/Second Light
49. ⛵ Michigan Island Old
50. ⛵ Outer Island
51. ⛵ Devil's Island
52. ⛵ Raspberry Island
53. ⛵ Sand Island
54. 🚗 Superior Entry South Breakwater/Wisconsin Point

41. Taken on 9-24-05

52. Taken on 9-25-05

# Minnesota

1. 🚗 Grand Marais
2. 🚗 Split Rock Point
3. 🚗 Two Harbors/Minnesota Light Station
4. 🚗 Two Harbors East Breakwater
5. 🚶 e  Duluth Harbor North Breakwater Pier
6. 🚶 e  Duluth South Breakwater Outer
7. 🚶 e  Duluth South Breakwater Inner
8. 🚶 h  Minnesota Point

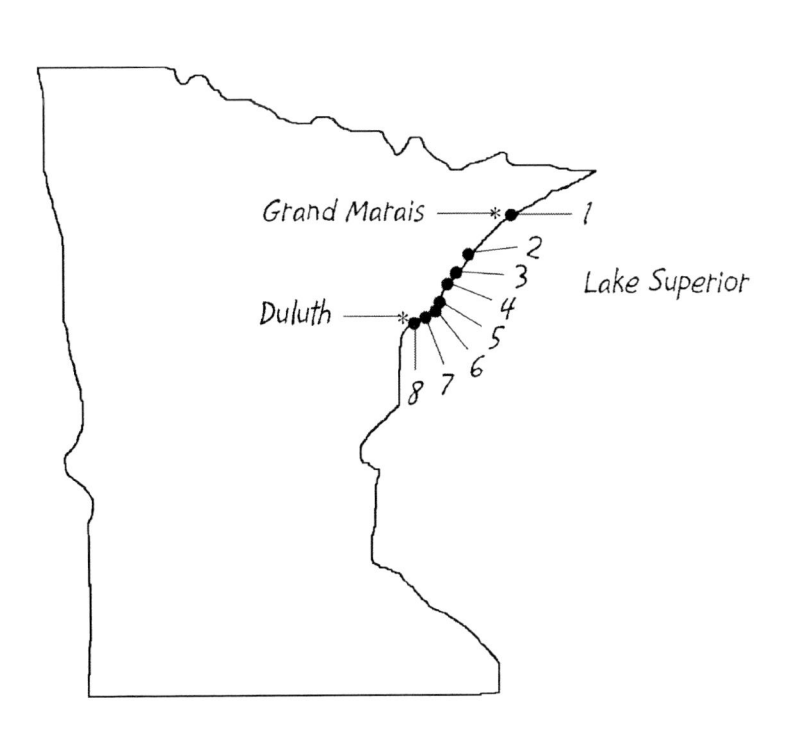

2. Taken on 9-24-01

3. Taken on 9-24-01

7. Taken on 9-23-01

# Alaska

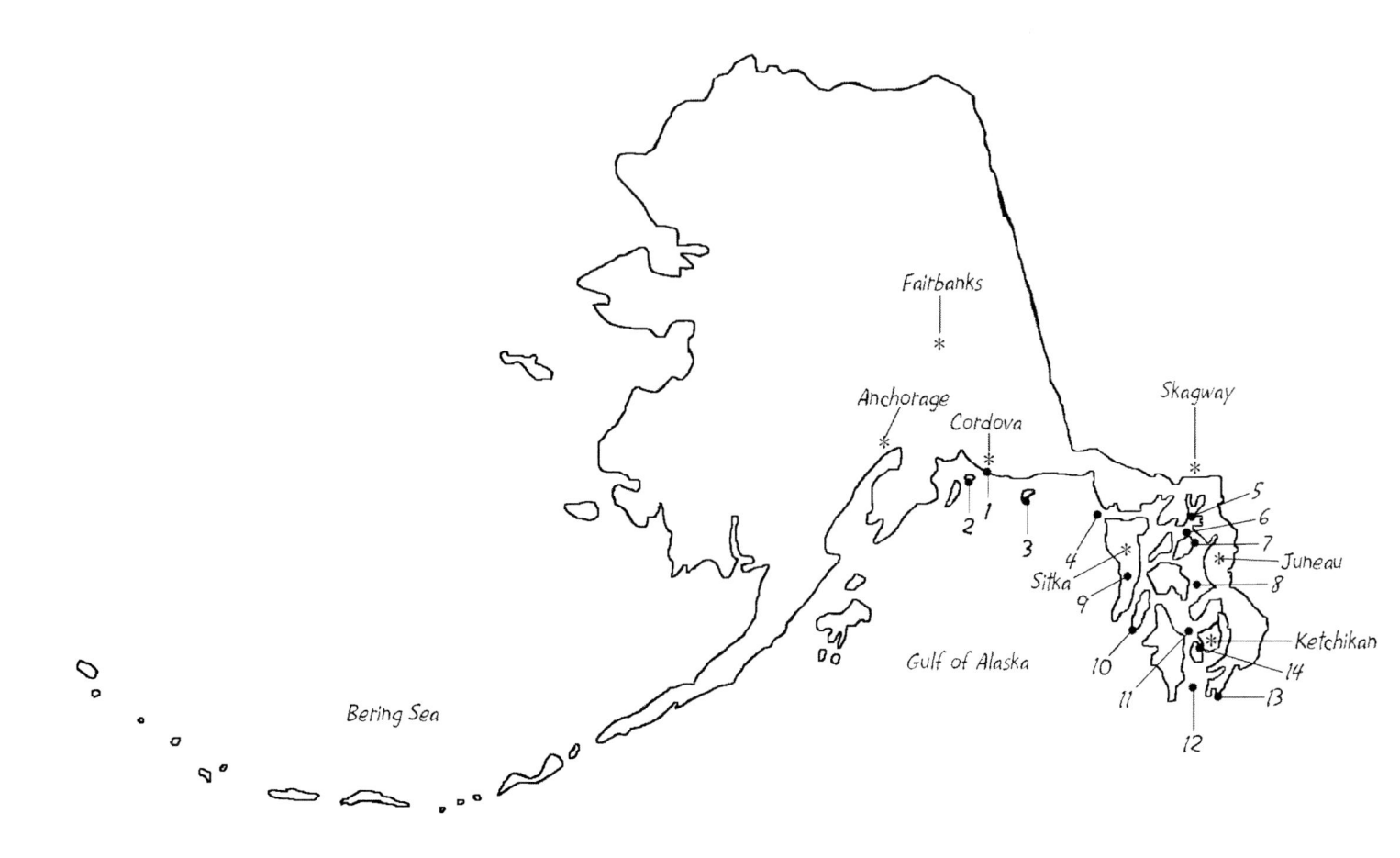

Fairbanks *

Anchorage *

Cordova *

Skagway *

Sitka *

Juneau *

Ketchikan *

Gulf of Alaska

Bering Sea

4.   Taken on 5-27-05

5.   Taken on 5-24-05

8.   Taken on 5-25-05

# Alaska

1. 🚗 Odiak Pharos
2. ✈ Cape Hinchenbrook
3. ✈ Cape St. Elias
4. ✈ Cape Spencer
5. ⛵ Eldred Rock
6. ⛵ Sentinal Island
7. ⛵ Point Retreat
8. ⛵ Five Fingers
9. 🚗 Rockwell
10. ✈ Cape Decision
11. ⛵ Guard Island
12. ✈ Mary Island
13. ✈ Tree Point
14. ⛵ Lightship Umatilla/WAL-196

3. Taken on 5-29-05

10. Taken on 6-2-05

# Washington

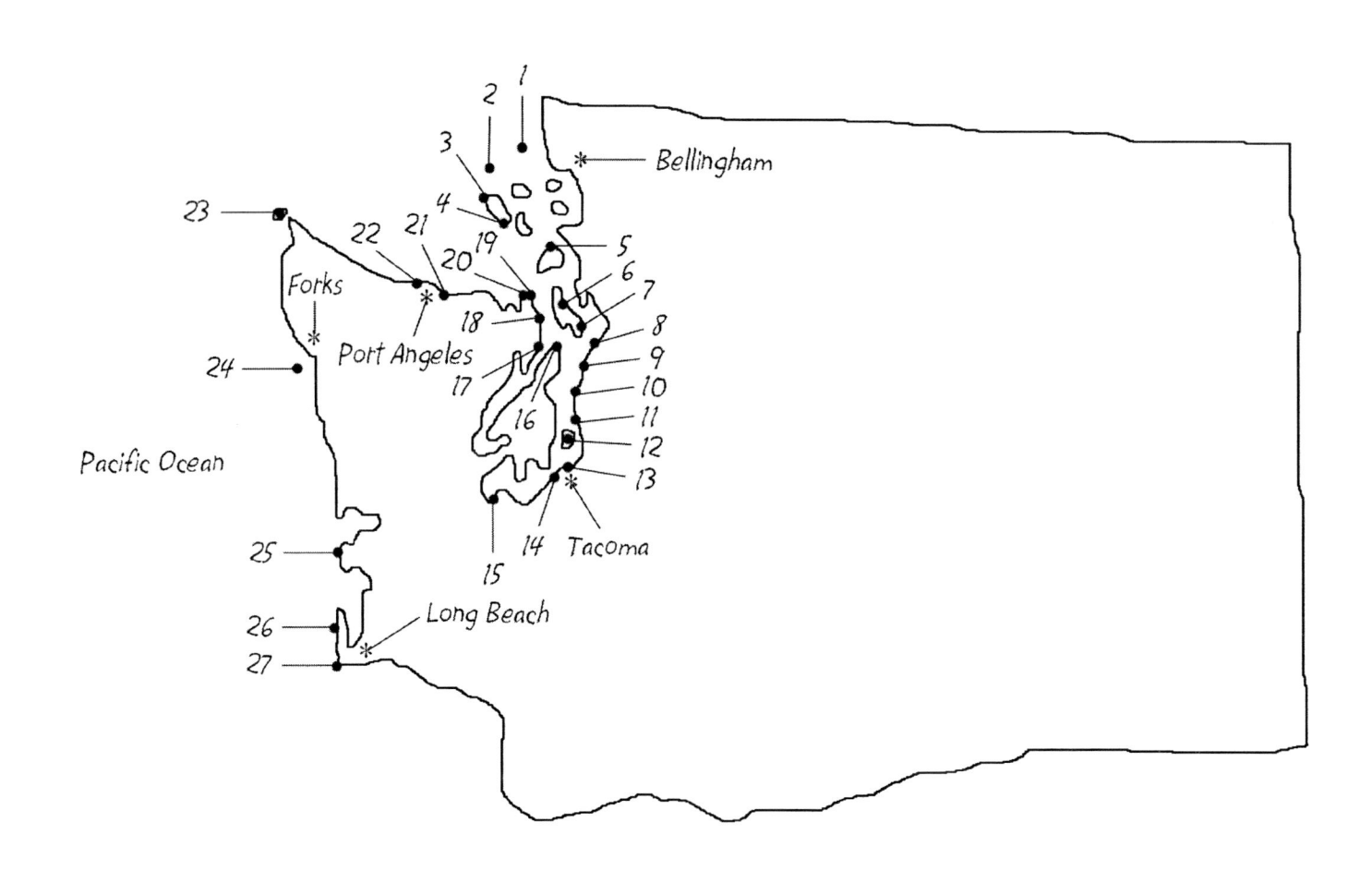

58

Bellingham

Forks

Port Angeles

Pacific Ocean

Tacoma

Long Beach

21.  Taken on 6-5-05         11.  Taken on 6-1-03         4.  Taken on 6-6-05

# Washington

1. ⛵ Patos Island
2. ⛵ Turn Point
3. ⛵ Lime Kiln
4. ⛵ Cattle Point
5. ⛵ Burrows Island
6. 🚗 Admiralty Head/Red Bluff
7. 🚗 Bush Point
8. 🚗 Mukilteo
9. 🚶 e West Point
10. 🚗 Lightship Swiftsure/LV-83/WAL-508
11. 🚗 Alki Point
12. 🚢 🚶 e Point Robinson
13. 🚶 e Gig Harbor
14. 🚗 Brown's Point
15. 🚗 Dofflemyer Point
16. 🚗 Skunk Bay
17. 🚗 Point No Point
18. 🚗 Marrowstone Point
19. 🚗 Dimick/Mukilteo Replica
20. 🚗 Point Wilson
21. 🚶 x New Dungeness
22. ⛵ Ediz Hook
23. 🚶 e Cape Flattery
24. ⛵ Destruction Island
25. 🚗 Gray's Harbor/Westport
26. 🚶 e North Head
27. 🚶 m Cape Disappointment

6. Taken on 6-2-03

23. Taken on 6-9-05

# Oregon

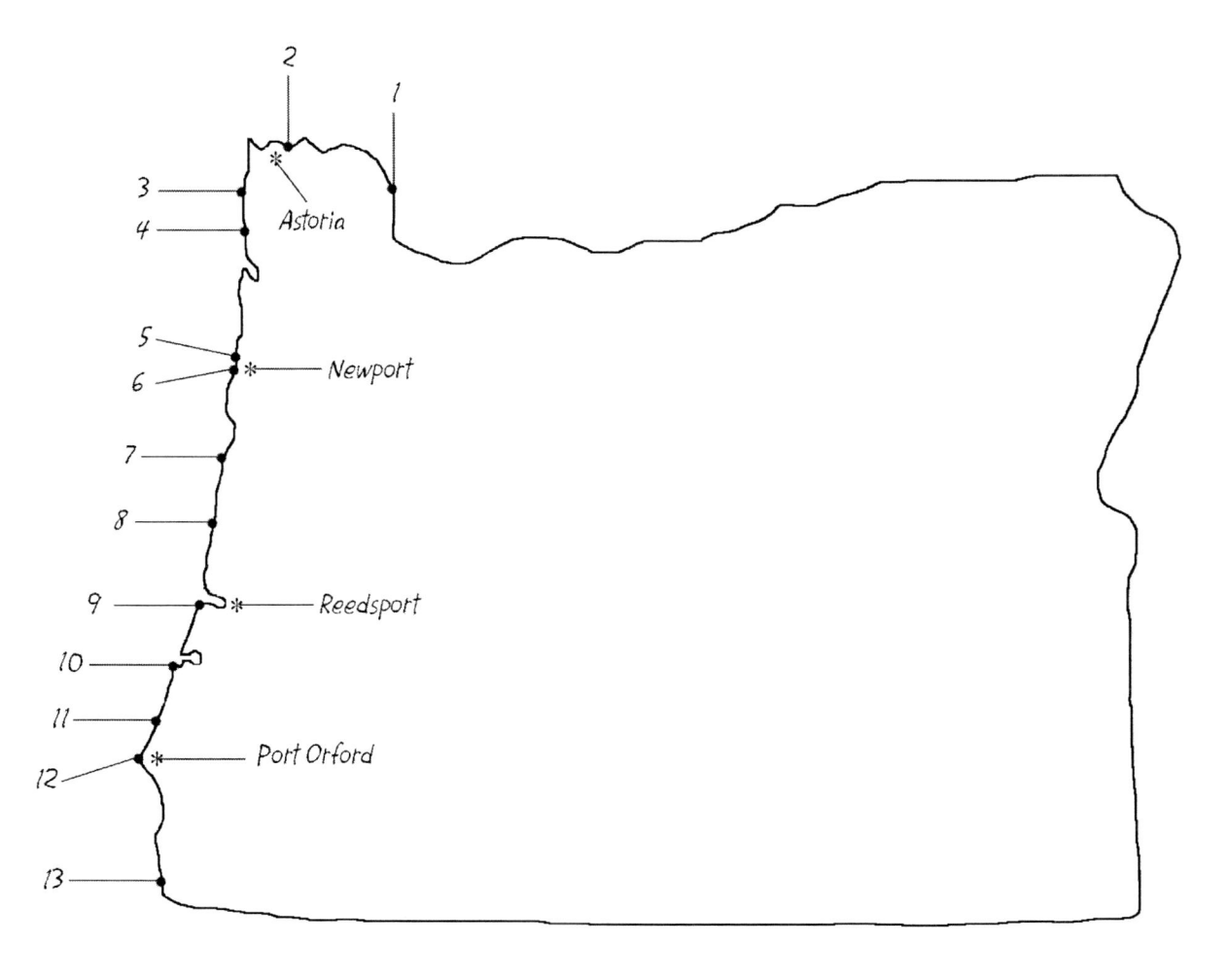

*Pacific Ocean*

1.
2.
3. Astoria
4.
5.
6. Newport
7.
8.
9. Reedsport
10.
11.
12. Port Orford
13.

5.  Taken on 6-10-03

3.  Taken on 6-11-03

8.  Taken on 6-10-03

## Oregon

1. 🚶 h  Warrior Rock
2. 🚗     Lightship Columbia/WLV-604
3. 🚗     Tillamook Rock/Terrible Tilly
4. 🚶 e  Cape Meares
5. 🚗     Yaquina Head
6. 🚗     Yaquina Bay
7. 🚗     Cleft on the Rock
8. 🚶 e  Heceta Head
9. 🚗     Umpqua River
10. 🚶 m Cape Arago
11. 🚗     Coquille River/Bandon
12. 🚶 m Cape Blanco
13. 🚗     Pelican Bay

1. Taken on 6-9-03

10. Taken on 6-6-06

# California

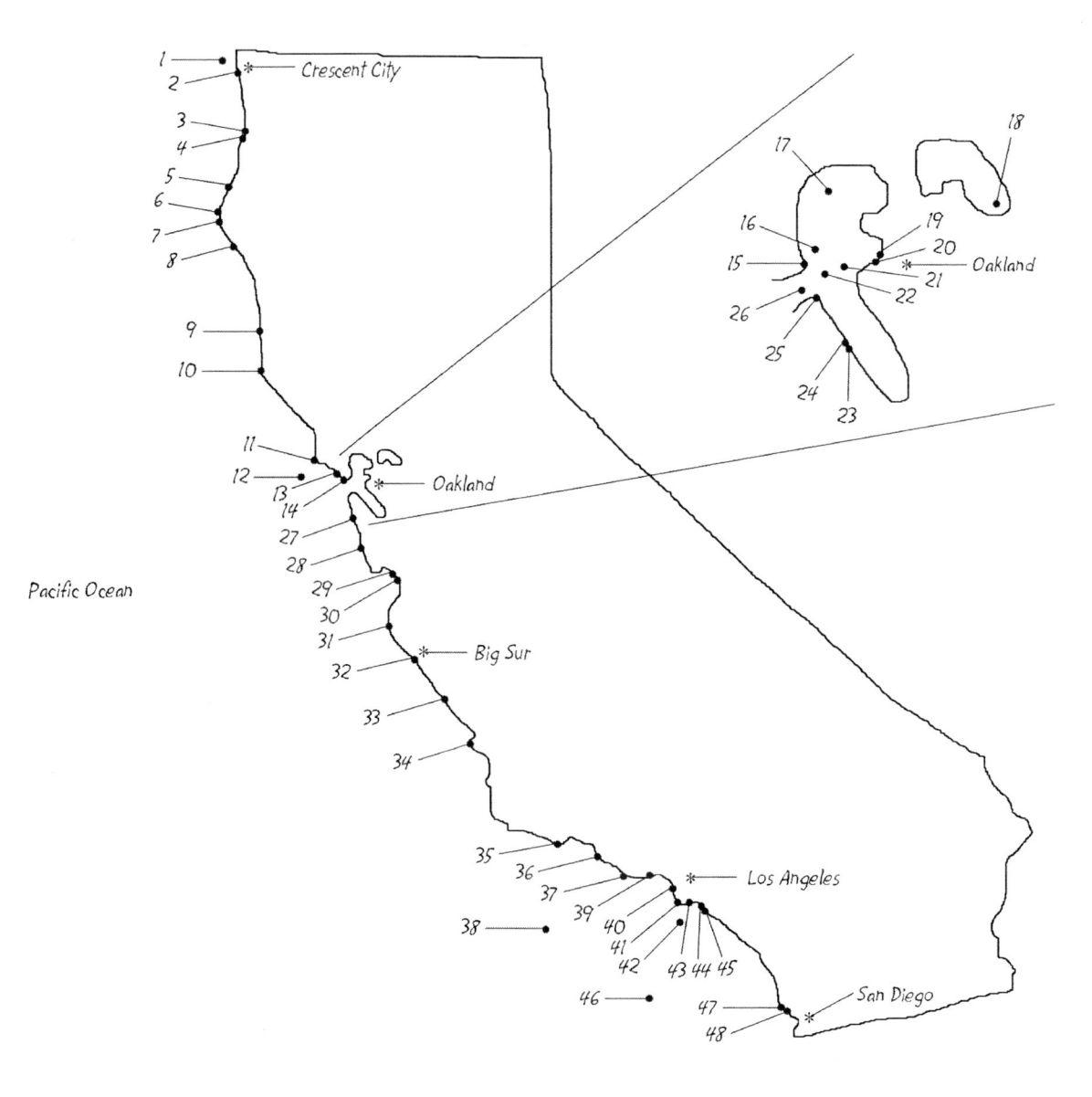

Crescent City

Oakland

Pacific Ocean

Big Sur

Los Angeles

San Diego

11.  Taken on 6-9-06      7.  Taken on 6-5-06      5.  Taken on 6-8-06

# California

1. ⛴ St. George Reef
2. 🚗 Battery Point/Crescent City
3. 🚗 Trinidad Head Memorial
4. ⛴ Trinidad Head
5. 🚗 Old Table Bluff/Table Bluff
6. 🚗 Cape Mendocino Replica
7. 🚗 Cape Mendocino/Shelter Cove
8. 🚶 x Punta Gorda
9. 🚶 e Point Cabrillo
10. 🚗 Point Arena
11. 🚶 m Point Reyes
12. ⛴ Farallon Islands
13. 🚶 m Point Bonita
14. ⛴ Point Diablo
15. 🚢 Lime Point
16. ⛴ Point Blunt/Angel Island
17. 🚗 East Brother
18. ⛴ Southampton Shoals
19. 🚗 Old Oakland Harbor
20. 🚗 Lightship Relief/WLV-605
21. 🚢 Yerba Buena/Goat Island
22. 🚢 Alcatraz Island
23. 🚗 Yacht Harbor fake
24. 🚗 Forbes Island fake
25. 🚗 Fort Point
26. ⛴ Mile Rocks
27. 🚗 Point Montara
28. 🚗 Pigeon Point
29. 🚗 Santa Cruz West Breakwater/Walton
30. 🚗 Santa Cruz/Mark Abbott Memorial
31. 🚗 Point Pinos
32. 🚶 m Point Sur
33. 🚗 Piedras Blancas
34. ⛴ Port San Luis/San Luis Obispo/Port Harford
35. ⛴ Point Conception
36. 🚗 Santa Barbara
37. 🚗 Oxnard fake
38. ⛴ Anacapa Island
39. 🚗 Point Hueneme

3. Taken on 6-15-02

8. Taken on 6-17-02

25. Taken on 6-20-02

## California continued

40. 🚗 Point Vicente
41. 🚗 Point Fermin
42. ⛵ Los Angeles Harbor/San Pedros Harbor/Angel's Gate
43. ⛵ Long Beach Harbor/Robot
44. 🚗 Long Beach/Lions Lighthouse for Sight
45. 🚗 Parker's
46. ⛵ Santa Barbara Island
47. 🚗 Old Point Loma
48. 🚗 Point Loma

47. Taken on 6-11-02

# Hawaii

1. 🚶 h   Kauhola Point/Kohala
2. 🚗     Coconut Point
3. 🚗     Cape Kumukahi
4. 🚗     Ka Lae/South Point
5. 🚗     McGregor Point
6. 🚗     Lahaina
7. ✈     Kalaupapa/Molokai
8. 🚶 h   Makapuu Point
9. 🚗     Diamond Head
10. 🚗    Aloha Tower
11. 🚗    Barber's Point
12. 🚗    Kileaua Point
13. 🚗    Nawiliwili Harbor
14. 🚶 e  Ninini Point

7. Taken on 7-13-04

12. Taken on 7-17-04

8. Taken on 7-23-04

## Ordering

Thank you for purchasing "**Lighthouses and Lightships of America--The Hunters Guide.**" We hope that you benefit from all of our years of hard work. We had a great time with all aspects of making this book. A special thank you goes out to Mrs. Sydney Koerner for her help with the proofreading of this and our future books. We also take photos of certain fake lighthouses and add them to our lists. We are working hard to make several lighthouse books with our color photos. If you would like to purchase any of our color photos from the lists in this book or other copies of our book please call us or use our web-site. Our web-site has many additional color photographs to choose from. We've seen over 1,000 lighthouses in the USA and Canada. You can also be added to our mailing list.

www.TheLighthouseHunters.com   Chris@TheLighthouseHunters.com

Most of our shots are in digital, while a few are still in 35 mm. I shoot a variety of shots so you can choose from either horizontal or vertical. I try to incorporate much of the scenery around the lighthouse for beautiful pictures. The photos you see on the web-site are in lesser quality than your prints will be. Just for the web-page we had to add our business name across the photo. Ask us about the photos you would like and we'll recommend if it's a suitable print. Let us know what your preference is; horizontal, vertical, very close, pretty close, farther away, or even just towers. We have all kinds to choose from. Your prints will be on quality photo paper. Tell us if you want just the photos or to have them mounted on a neutral colored mat.

Prints of
- 3 ½" x 7" with a 5" x 7" natural color mat
- 5" x 7" with an 8" x 10" natural color mat
- 8" x 10" with an 11" x 14" natural color mat
- 11" x 14" with a 16" x 20" natural color mat

(Shipping charges will be lower on multiple photos sent in one package.)
Orders will be filled in 2-3 weeks and mailed by the US Postal Service.
We both still are working at our full time jobs and still go out to re-shoot lighthouses.
We're always trying to improve our shots.

Christine & Thomas Cardaci    12 Central Avenue Highlands, NJ 07732    732-291-2710
1st Edition, November 2005©
Copyright 2005, by Christine and Thomas Cardaci

ISBN 978-0-9777687-0-7

All rights reserved. No part of this book may be reproduced or transmitted in any form by any means, electronic or mechanical, including photocopying and recording, or by any information storage and retrieval systems, except as may be expressly permitted by the 1976 Copyright Act or by the publisher. Requests for permission should be made in writing to:
Christine and Thomas Cardaci    12 Central Avenue    Highlands, NJ    07732-1406

## References

We have read a few lighthouse books over the years for our lighthouse adventures. We use the local state and providence maps to help pinpoint the lighthouses. Sometimes there are even lighthouse symbols on the maps. We also use the lighthouse information we are given from the areas or lighthouses themselves. One of the best places to find out information on an individual lighthouse is on-line with the Lighthouse Digest. They have been very helpful once I began going on-line. Too bad I started so late using that because it could have saved me lots of time while on some earlier vacations. Another great tool we used was the maps from the Hartnett House Map Publishers. They make great maps filled with information and they pinpoint exactly where the lights are for you. They still have many more maps to make. You can even hang the laminated maps on the wall like we did.

Please become a member of the American Lighthouse Foundation-ALF and some of the other lighthouse societies. Another way to help is by subscribing to the Lighthouse Digest. With your support they can help to preserve the lighthouses for future generations.

Lighthouse Digest Magazine and www.lhdigest.com

Hartnett House Map Publishers--www.hartnetthouse.com

<u>Great Lakes Lighthouses American & Canadian</u>, Wes Oleszewski, Avery Color Studios, Inc., 1998
<u>America's Atlantic Coast Lighthouses</u>, Kenneth G. Kochel, Kenneth Kochel Publishing, 1998
<u>List of All Existing U.S. Lighthouses</u>, Bob & Sandra Shanklin, Bob & Sandra Shanklin, 2003
<u>Southern Lighthouses</u>, Bruce Roberts & Ray Jones, The Globe Pequot Press, 2002
<u>Gulf Coast Lighthouses</u>, Bruce Roberts & Ray Jones, The Globe Pequot Press, 1998
<u>A Traveler's Guide to 116 Western Great Lakes Lighthouses</u>, Penrose, Friede Publications, 1995
<u>A Traveler's Guide to 100 Eastern Great Lakes Lighthouses</u>, Penrose, Friede Publications, 1994
<u>Lighthouses of the Pacific Coast</u>, Randy Leffingwell & Pamela Welty, Voyageur Press, Inc., 2000

To Judy,
Happy Hunting!
Chris Cardaci

*Happy hunting from The Lighthouse Hunters--Christine and Tommy Cardaci*

## Order & Mailing List

Please print out this order form. Then clearly fill out this order form and mail it to us with your payment of personal check, cashiers check, or money order. Sorry no credit cards will be accepted at this time. You may call us at home to place an order at 732-291-2710
The Lighthouse Hunters Christine & Tommy Cardaci 12 Central Avenue Highlands, NJ 07732-1406
We will put you on our mailing list so we can keep you updated on our future lighthouse books.

First Name:
Last Name:
Address:
City:
State:                                          Zip Code:
Phone Number:                                   E-mail Address:
Address to be mailed to if different:
Comments:

Please list below exactly what you would like to purchase; the book and/or color photographs.

This USA book "Lighthouses and Lightships of America--The Hunters Guide"

The color lighthouse photographs are to be listed with the state name & the name of the lighthouse. Choose what you want, either a horizontal shot or a vertical shot. Then choose the size of the color photo and if you want that photo to be placed in a natural colored mat.
Example: AK--Point Retreat Lighthouse, Horizontal, 8" x 10" print in an 11" x 14" mat
All New Jersey residents will have to add the 7% sales tax.
Shipping & handling prices will vary.
Please check our website for up to date prices.

1.
2.
3.
4.
5.
6.
7.
8.
9.
10.
11.
12.